the book of

job

authorised king james version

printed by authority

published by canongate

with an introduction by | louis de bernières

First published in Great Britain in 1998
by Canongate Books Ltd
14 High Street, Edinburgh EH1 1TE

10 9 8 7 6 5 4 3 2

British Library Cataloguing-in-Publication Data
A catalogue record is available on request from
the British Library

ISBN 0 86241 791 0

Typeset by Palimpsest Book Production
Book design by Paddy Cramsie
Printed and bound in Great Britain
by Caledonian International, Bishopbriggs

a note about pocket canons

The Authorised King James Version of the Bible, translated between 1603–11, coincided with an extraordinary flowering of English literature. This version, more than any other, and possibly more than any other work in history, has had an influence in shaping the language we speak and write today. Presenting individual books from the Bible as separate volumes, as they were originally conceived, encourages the reader to approach them as literary works in their own right.

The first twelve books in this series encompass categories as diverse as history, fiction, philosophy, love poetry and law. Each Pocket Canon also has its own introduction, specially commissioned from an impressive range of writers, which provides a personal interpretation of the text and explores its contemporary relevance.

Louis de Bernières's first three novels are The War of Don Emmanuel's Nether Parts, Señor Vivo and the Coca Lord *and* The Troublesome Offspring of Cardinal Guzman. *His last book,* Captain Corelli's Mandolin, *is now a major best-seller worldwide and it won the Commonwealth Writers' Prize, Best Book, in 1995. Louis de Bernières lives in London.*

introduction by louis de bernières:
the impatience of job

One would naturally assume that a book of the Old Testament must have been written by an Israelite, and indeed the earliest rabbinical tradition asserts that Moses was the author of *The Book of Job*. In the past Christians readily accepted this notion, which is why, for example, one finds Isaak Walton referring to it whilst discoursing on the alleged patience of the angler. In fact there are literary parallels to the story in Persian, Sumerian, Akkadian and Babylonian, and in the Biblical version there appear to be several allusions to Ugaritic myth. Some of the unique or rare words in the text are possibly Edomite. There exists an apocryphal 'Testament of Job', and there is even an amusing tale about Job and his wife in the Islamic tradition. It would seem, then, that the story is a variant on an ancient folktale, that may indeed be as old as the patriarchs, but could have been composed by anyone from any of the interlocking mosaic of cultures that existed in the region between 2000 and 700 BCE. God, in the story, is not omniscient (He asks Satan what he has been up to), there is no clear belief in the afterlife, and Satan is still one of God's courtiers. This means that if the tale is Jewish, it would have to date from before the exile in Babylon.

There may have been at least three authors of the book,

since Elihu's intervention, and the long and wonderful poem about the inaccessibility of wisdom are almost certainly interpolations, but whoever the main author was, he was a great poet. The original is very terse, but since Hebrew requires half the number of words needed in English, no English translation could hope to do justice to it. Furthermore, no-one knows exactly how Hebrew poetry was stressed or scanned, and so for us the quality of the verse will depend upon the force, aptness and beauty of expression; the reader of *Job* will be struck mostly by the skill of the author in repeating the same thoughts in new ways that are continually refreshing and illuminating. It has to be said that one gains very little new information from each speech, and anyone looking for snappy action and exciting new events would certainly be better off hiring a video, the point being that this is really a long and beautiful poem about divine justice, rendered in the forms of narrative, dialogue, hymn, lament, proverb, and oracle. The compilers of the King James version in this volume did not have the benefit of modern scholarship, and so their rendition is often confused and inaccurate, but they have nonetheless managed to contribute their sonorously fair share of poetry to the English language. Chapter 14 stands independently as a moving lament for the human condition: 'Man that is born of a woman is of few days, and full of trouble. He cometh forth like a flower, and is cut down …'.

Elsewhere we find the proverbs: 'The price of wisdom is above rubies' and 'The fear of the Lord, that is wisdom', and the memorable words adapted by Handel for his *Messiah*: 'I know that my redeemer liveth, and that he shall stand at the latter day upon the earth; and though after my skin worms destroy this body, yet in my flesh shall I see God.' It may be unfortunate that this is a hopeless mistranslation of the original verses, which are not about redemption and resurrection at all, but it is still great writing.

The book is in fact very largely about faith, however, and particularly about the issue of theodicy – whether or not one can have faith in the goodness and worthiness of an omnipotent creator who is apparently responsible for creating evil, and tolerating the suffering of the innocent. Whereas Job's attitude is profoundly felt and deeply personal, his four comforters take a more detached and philosophical line, but it is important to remember that God and Satan are the only two who really know what is going on.

Satan is portrayed as an affable but astute fellow who is on terms of familiarity with God; when the latter asks him where he has been, Satan casually replies 'From going to and fro in the earth, and from walking up and down in it.' When God invites Satan to admire Job's uprightness, Satan very acutely points out that God has made sure that Job has had an easy ride of it, 'but put forth thine hand now, and touch all he hath, and he will curse thee to thy face.' God accepts the challenge, with the proviso that Job himself must not be physically harmed, whereupon Satan destroys Job's oxen, sheep, camels, servants and children. Job's equanimity survives these trials, and Satan points out to God that an attack on Job's person is more likely to do the trick. God gives his permission, and Job is struck down by a revolting combination of foul diseases. At this point Job does indeed turn against God, and Satan is heard of no more, having won his wager. The quantity of shekels involved in this bet is not recorded, but no doubt Satan spends them whilst going once more to and fro in the earth, and walking up and down in it, his conscience eased by the thought that he has merely been obeying orders from a superior.

Job's comforters are possibly the most irritating characters in all of literature, and Job more than once tells them that they are completely intolerable. Elihu is the last, and is the most annoying of all of them, since he announces that all the others have been beside the point, whilst he, although the youngest, has the conclusive arguments. He then says nothing interesting or original, in the manner of sententious bores the world over. He says that God rescues people repeatedly, that it is up to God to choose what happens, that Job must have done something wrong, because God is righteous, that God is beyond our capacity to comprehend, and that God does not do evil.

To be fair to young Elihu, he was probably not in the original story, but the other self-righteous prigs certainly were. Each has three speeches, and Job replies to them in turn. Eliphaz says that God only punishes the wicked, that God saves and protects, that we cannot know God's plans, that Man is naturally vile and unclean in God's eyes, that God punishes sinners in their own lifetime, and that Job must therefore be a rebel and a sinner. His concluding comment is that none of us make any difference to God one way or the other.

Bildad asserts that God does not pervert justice, that we

are ignorant of the real state of things, that God will not reject the upright, that we are punished for forgetting God, and that Job must therefore be evil and Godless. His final thought is that we are nothing, before God's omnipotence.

Zophar says that God knows what the reality is, and that therefore Job must be guilty of something. The mirth of the wicked is brief, he says, and God brings them down.

That phrase about the 'patience of Job' could not be further from the mark. Job is, for all but three of the forty-two chapters, exasperated by his comforters, reduced to abject misery by his afflictions, and disillusioned and furious with God. 'The defiance of Job' would have been a far more apposite figure of speech to have passed into the language. His comforters have all the usual inane, pious, platitudinous, facile morsels of cod-wisdom at their fingertips, but it is Job who has all the passion, and all the grasp of the real paradoxes implicit in the idea of theodicy. Job tells his comforters that his argument is with God, and not with them, and that, if they are just trying to curry favour with God, then the latter will surely see through them. He says that in their position he would talk the same rot. He even accuses them of behaving like God, and persecuting him unjustly. Readers, of course, are in the privileged position of knowing that all the arguments of the comforters are either false or completely beside the point, since God's assault on Job is nothing whatsoever to do with just punishment, it is to do with an interesting bet between Himself and one of His friends.

louis de bernières

There is an amusing vignette, wherein Job's wife advises him to curse God and die, whereupon he says, 'Thou speakest as one of the foolish women speaketh.' Before long, however, he is indeed cursing God and wishing for death, and no doubt Mrs Job (whose name was said to be 'Sitis') derives some quiet satisfaction from this. Chrysostom proposed that Mrs Job might have been Job's 'greatest scourge of all', but this would seem to reflect the former's peculiar preoccupations rather than anything one can find in the story. Job is very like the character of Philoctetes in the play of Sophocles, abandoned on an island whilst his foot rots, and his sentiments are very much those of Jesus on the cross, who cries out, 'My God, My God, why has thou forsaken me?' There is also a remarkable but probably coincidental resemblance between Job's declarations of innocence and the speech of the dead before Osiris in the Hall of Righteousness, as inscribed in the Egyptian 'Chapters of Coming Forth by Day' (*The Book of the Dead*).

Job reproaches God, saying, 'They are tricked that trusted.' He avows ignorance of any wrongdoing on his part, and he demands how is one supposed to have a sensible argument with God when the latter is omnipotent, invisible, unaccountable, and unjust? It is futile asserting one's right when God is both adversary, judge, and executioner, and why does God take vicious action against that which he has created? God is an oppressor, He is incapable of human sympathy; behind a smiling face He hides an evil heart. Job asks why we bother to serve God; the wicked prosper, He does nothing to help the desperate ('God thinks nothing amiss'). Job's despair is so well depicted that we get a distinct and lasting impression of his character, the most notable feature of which is his absolute refusal to disengage his intelligence, be a hypocrite, or give up his case. He is not going to be cowed even by fear of God or by the untrue accusations of his friends. This makes Job a very modern figure (in literature if not in real life), one who asserts his individuality and integrity in the face of all conventional wisdom or arbitrary power. He is, in other words, a classic existentialist hero.

At the end of the tale there is a theophany, God speaks out of the whirlwind, and demonstrates, to His credit, that he finds the comforters as tiresome and obnoxious as Job does. He reproves them: 'My wrath is kindled against thee … for ye have not spoken of me the thing that is right, as my servant Job hath.' It is rather startling to find God thus admitting somewhat disarmingly to all of Job's indictments, but it is true even so that He comes out of this story as the most morally tarnished. The comforters may emerge from it looking stupid (which they are), but God does so looking like an unpleasantly sarcastic megalomaniac. Instead of answering Job's charges of injustice and heartlessness, God devotes 129 verses to a magnificently irrelevant and bombastic speech about His own accomplishments and abilities; it is as if He knows perfectly well that He has abused His power, but does not wish to address the issue. God boasts about two of his favourite and most impressive creations, Behemoth and Leviathan, but at no point does He clear up the mystery that we call 'The Problem of Evil'. We are left with Job holding the field philosophically, with no-one to deny that God finds nothing amiss, and would not care even if He did.

It is true that God restores Job to good health and good fortune, but He absentmindedly does not restore to life the servants or the children killed off in chapter 1; they get no justice. Not only do we have a God, therefore, who is a frivolous trickster, but one who even botches up the reparations when He decides to make them. There are many episodes in the Bible that show God in a very bad light, such as when he commands Abraham to sacrifice his son Isaac, or when He commands Saul to destroy the Amalekites ('... Utterly destroy all that they have, and spare them not; but slay both man and woman, infant and suckling, ox and sheep, camel and ass'), and one cannot but conclude from them either that God is a mad, bloodthirsty, and capricious despot, or that all this time we have been inadvertently worshipping the Devil.

In the modern age in the West there has been a great falling off of religious faith, because although Jesus Christ and a deluge of sophistical theology did much to improve God's image for a few centuries, Job is still winning the argument, and *The Book of Job* is still insidiously subversive. If God is omnipotent, we cannot blame anything on the Devil, and if God is no help, we have to do His work for Him. He has still failed to appear in court, and we construe His absence either as non-existence, hubris, apathy, or an admission of guilt. We miss Him, we would dearly like to see Him going to and fro in the earth and walking up and down in it, but we admire tyranny no longer, and we desire justice more than we are awed by vainglorious asseverations of magnificence.

the book of job

There was a man in the land of Uz, whose name was Job;
and that man was perfect and upright, and one that feared
God, and eschewed evil. ²And there were born unto him
seven sons and three daughters. ³His substance also was
seven thousand sheep, and three thousand camels, and five
hundred yoke of oxen, and five hundred she asses, and a very
great household; so that this man was the greatest of all the
men of the east. ⁴And his sons went and feasted in their
houses, every one his day; and sent and called for their three
sisters to eat and to drink with them. ⁵And it was so, when
the days of their feasting were gone about, that Job sent and
sanctified them, and rose up early in the morning, and offered
burnt offerings according to the number of them all: for Job
said, 'It may be that my sons have sinned, and cursed God in
their hearts.' Thus did Job continually.

⁶Now there was a day when the sons of God came to
present themselves before the Lord, and Satan came also
among them. ⁷And the Lord said unto Satan, 'Whence comest
thou?' Then Satan answered the Lord, and said, 'From going
to and fro in the earth, and from walking up and down in it.'
⁸And the Lord said unto Satan, 'Hast thou considered my servant Job, that there is none like him in the earth, a perfect

and an upright man, one that feareth God, and escheweth evil?' ⁹Then Satan answered the Lord, and said, 'Doth Job fear God for nought? ¹⁰Hast not thou made an hedge about him, and about his house, and about all that he hath on every side? Thou hast blessed the work of his hands, and his substance is increased in the land. ¹¹But put forth thine hand now, and touch all that he hath, and he will curse thee to thy face.' ¹²And the Lord said unto Satan, 'Behold, all that he hath is in thy power; only upon himself put not forth thine hand.' So Satan went forth from the presence of the Lord.

¹³And there was a day when his sons and his daughters were eating and drinking wine in their eldest brother's house, ¹⁴and there came a messenger unto Job, and said, 'The oxen were plowing, and the asses feeding beside them; ¹⁵and the Sabeans fell upon them, and took them away; yea, they have slain the servants with the edge of the sword; and I only am escaped alone to tell thee.' ¹⁶While he was yet speaking, there came also another, and said, 'The fire of God is fallen from heaven, and hath burned up the sheep, and the servants, and consumed them; and I only am escaped alone to tell thee.' ¹⁷While he was yet speaking, there came also another, and said, 'The Chaldeans made out three bands, and fell upon the camels, and have carried them away, yea, and slain the servants with the edge of the sword; and I only am escaped alone to tell thee.' ¹⁸While he was yet speaking, there came also another, and said, 'Thy sons and thy daughters were eating and drinking wine in their eldest brother's house; ¹⁹and, behold, there came a great wind from the wilderness, and

smote the four corners of the house, and it fell upon the young men, and they are dead; and I only am escaped alone to tell thee.' [20] Then Job arose, and rent his mantle, and shaved his head, and fell down upon the ground, and worshipped, [21] and said,

> 'Naked came I out of my mother's womb,
>> and naked shall I return thither:
>>> the Lord gave, and the Lord hath taken away;
>>> blessed be the name of the Lord.'

[22] In all this Job sinned not, nor charged God foolishly.

2 Again there was a day when the sons of God came to present themselves before the Lord, and Satan came also among them to present himself before the Lord. [2] And the Lord said unto Satan, 'From whence comest thou?' And Satan answered the Lord, and said, 'From going to and fro in the earth, and from walking up and down in it.' [3] And the Lord said unto Satan, 'Hast thou considered my servant Job, that there is none like him in the earth, a perfect and an upright man, one that feareth God, and escheweth evil? And still he holdeth fast his integrity, although thou movedst me against him, to destroy him without cause.' [4] And Satan answered the Lord, and said, 'Skin for skin, yea, all that a man hath will he give for his life. [5] But put forth thine hand now, and touch his bone and his flesh, and he will curse thee to thy face.' [6] And the Lord said unto Satan, 'Behold, he is in thine hand; but save his life.'

⁷So went Satan forth from the presence of the Lord, and smote Job with sore boils from the sole of his foot unto his crown. ⁸And he took him a potsherd to scrape himself withal; and he sat down among the ashes.

⁹Then said his wife unto him, 'Dost thou still retain thine integrity? Curse God, and die.' ¹⁰But he said unto her, 'Thou speakest as one of the foolish women speaketh. What? Shall we receive good at the hand of God, and shall we not receive evil?' In all this did not Job sin with his lips.

¹¹Now when Job's three friends heard of all this evil that was come upon him, they came every one from his own place: Eliphaz the Temanite, and Bildad the Shuhite, and Zophar the Naamathite; for they had made an appointment together to come to mourn with him and to comfort him. ¹²And when they lifted up their eyes afar off, and knew him not, they lifted up their voice, and wept; and they rent every one his mantle, and sprinkled dust upon their heads toward heaven. ¹³So they sat down with him upon the ground seven days and seven nights, and none spake a word unto him: for they saw that his grief was very great.

3 After this opened Job his mouth, and cursed his day. ²And Job spake, and said,

> ³'Let the day perish wherein I was born,
>   and the night in which it was said,
>   "There is a man child conceived."
> ⁴Let that day be darkness;

let not God regard it from above,
>   neither let the light shine upon it.
5 Let darkness and the shadow of death stain it;
>   let a cloud dwell upon it;
>   let the blackness of the day terrify it.
6 As for that night, let darkness seize upon it;
>   let it not be joined unto the days of the year;
>   let it not come into the number of the months.
7 Lo, let that night be solitary,
>   let no joyful voice come therein.
8 Let them curse it that curse the day,
>   who are ready to raise up their mourning.
9 Let the stars of the twilight thereof be dark;
>   let it look for light, but have none;
>   neither let it see the dawning of the day:
10 because it shut not up the doors of my mother's
>   womb, nor hid sorrow from mine eyes.
11 Why died I not from the womb?
>   why did I not give up the ghost
>   when I came out of the belly?
12 Why did the knees prevent me?
>   Or why the breasts that I should suck?
13 For now should I have lain still and been quiet,
>   I should have slept: then had I been at rest,
14 with kings and counsellors of the earth,
>   which built desolate places for themselves;
15 or with princes that had gold,
>   who filled their houses with silver:

[16] or as an hidden untimely birth I had not been;
  as infants which never saw light.
[17] There the wicked cease from troubling;
  and there the weary be at rest.
[18] There the prisoners rest together;
  they hear not the voice of the oppressor.
[19] The small and great are there;
  and the servant is free from his master.
[20] Wherefore is light given to him that is in misery,
  and life unto the bitter in soul;
[21] which long for death, but it cometh not,
  and dig for it more than for hid treasures;
[22] which rejoice exceedingly, and are glad,
  when they can find the grave?
[23] Why is light given to a man whose way is hid,
  and whom God hath hedged in?
[24] For my sighing cometh before I eat,
  and my roarings are poured out like the waters.
[25] For the thing which I greatly feared
  is come upon me, and that
    which I was afraid of is come unto me.
[26] I was not in safety, neither had I rest,
  neither was I quiet; yet trouble came.'

4 Then Eliphaz the Temanite answered and said, [2] 'If we assay to commune with thee, wilt thou be grieved? But who can withhold himself from speaking? [3] Behold, thou hast instructed many, and thou hast strengthened the weak hands.

⁴ Thy words have upholden him that was falling, and thou hast strengthened the feeble knees. ⁵ But now it is come upon thee, and thou faintest; it toucheth thee, and thou art troubled. ⁶ Is not this thy fear, thy confidence, thy hope, and the uprightness of thy ways? ⁷ Remember, I pray thee, who ever perished, being innocent? Or where were the righteous cut off? ⁸ Even as I have seen, they that plow iniquity, and sow wickedness, reap the same. ⁹ By the blast of God they perish, and by the breath of his nostrils are they consumed. ¹⁰ The roaring of the lion, and the voice of the fierce lion, and the teeth of the young lions, are broken. ¹¹ The old lion perisheth for lack of prey, and the stout lion's whelps are scattered abroad. ¹² Now a thing was secretly brought to me, and mine ear received a little thereof. ¹³ In thoughts from the visions of the night, when deep sleep falleth on men, ¹⁴ fear came upon me, and trembling, which made all my bones to shake. ¹⁵ Then a spirit passed before my face; the hair of my flesh stood up. ¹⁶ It stood still, but I could not discern the form thereof: an image was before mine eyes, there was silence, and I heard a voice, saying, ¹⁷ "Shall mortal man be more just than God? Shall a man be more pure than his maker? ¹⁸ Behold, he put no trust in his servants; and his angels he charged with folly; ¹⁹ how much less in them that dwell in houses of clay, whose foundation is in the dust, which are crushed before the moth? ²⁰ They are destroyed from morning to evening; they perish for ever without any regarding it. ²¹ Doth not their excellency which is in them go away? They die, even without wisdom."'

5 'Call now, if there be any that will answer thee; and to which of the saints wilt thou turn? ²For wrath killeth the foolish man, and envy slayeth the silly one. ³I have seen the foolish taking root; but suddenly I cursed his habitation. ⁴His children are far from safety, and they are crushed in the gate, neither is there any to deliver them. ⁵Whose harvest the hungry eateth up, and taketh it even out of the thorns, and the robber swalloweth up their substance. ⁶Although affliction cometh not forth of the dust, neither doth trouble spring out of the ground; ⁷yet man is born unto trouble, as the sparks fly upward. ⁸I would seek unto God, and unto God would I commit my cause: ⁹which doeth great things and unsearchable, marvellous things without number; ¹⁰who giveth rain upon the earth, and sendeth waters upon the fields; ¹¹to set up on high those that be low, that those which mourn may be exalted to safety. ¹²He disappointeth the devices of the crafty, so that their hands cannot perform their enterprise. ¹³He taketh the wise in their own craftiness; and the counsel of the forward is carried headlong. ¹⁴They meet with darkness in the daytime, and grope in the noonday as in the night. ¹⁵But he saveth the poor from the sword, from their mouth, and from the hand of the mighty. ¹⁶So the poor hath hope, and iniquity stoppeth her mouth. ¹⁷Behold, happy is the man whom God correcteth; therefore despise not thou the chastening of the Almighty: ¹⁸for he maketh sore, and bindeth up; he woundeth, and his hands make whole. ¹⁹He shall deliver thee in six troubles; yea, in seven there shall no evil touch thee. ²⁰In famine he shall redeem thee from death;

and in war from the power of the sword. ²¹ Thou shalt be hid
from the scourge of the tongue; neither shalt thou be afraid
of destruction when it cometh. ²²At destruction and famine
thou shalt laugh; neither shalt thou be afraid of the beasts
of the earth. ²³ For thou shalt be in league with the stones of
the field; and the beasts of the field shall be at peace with
thee. ²⁴And thou shalt know that thy tabernacle shall be in
peace; and thou shalt visit thy habitation, and shalt not sin.
²⁵ Thou shalt know also that thy seed shall be great, and thine
offspring as the grass of the earth. ²⁶ Thou shalt come to thy
grave in a full age, like as a shock of corn cometh in his season. ²⁷ Lo this, we have searched it, so it is; hear it, and know
thou it for thy good.'

6 But Job answered and said,

²'Oh that my grief were throughly weighed,
    and my calamity laid in the balances together!
³ For now it would be heavier
    than the sand of the sea;
        therefore my words are swallowed up.
⁴ For the arrows of the Almighty are within me,
    the poison whereof drinketh up my spirit:
        the terrors of God do set themselves
        in array against me.
⁵ Doth the wild ass bray when he hath grass?
    Or loweth the ox over his fodder?
⁶ Can that which is unsavoury be eaten without salt?

Or is there any taste in the white of an egg?
⁷ The things that my soul refused to touch
   are as my sorrowful meat.
⁸ Oh that I might have my request; and that
   God would grant me the thing that I long for!
⁹ Even that it would please God to destroy me;
   that he would let loose his hand, and cut me off!
¹⁰ Then should I yet have comfort;
   yea, I would harden myself in sorrow:
      let him not spare; for I have not concealed
   the words of the Holy One.
¹¹ What is my strength, that I should hope?
   And what is mine end,
      that I should prolong my life?
¹² Is my strength the strength of stones?
   Or is my flesh of brass?
¹³ Is not my help in me?
   And is wisdom driven quite from me?
¹⁴ To him that is afflicted pity
   should be shewed from his friend;
      but he forsaketh the fear of the Almighty.
¹⁵ My brethren have dealt deceitfully as a brook,
   and as the stream of brooks they pass away;
¹⁶ which are blackish by reason of the ice,
   and wherein the snow is hid.
¹⁷ What time they wax warm, they vanish;
   when it is hot,
      they are consumed out of their place.

¹⁸ The paths of their way are turned aside;
    they go to nothing, and perish.
¹⁹ The troops of Tema looked,
    the companies of Sheba waited for them.
²⁰ They were confounded because they had hoped;
    they came thither, and were ashamed.
²¹ For now ye are nothing;
    ye see my casting down, and are afraid.
²² Did I say, "Bring unto me?"
    or, "Give a reward for me of your substance?"
²³ or, "Deliver me from the enemy's hand?"
    or, "Redeem me from the hand of the mighty?"
²⁴ Teach me, and I will hold my tongue;
    and cause me to understand
        wherein I have erred.
²⁵ How forcible are right words!
    But what doth your arguing reprove?
²⁶ Do ye imagine to reprove words,
    and the speeches of one that is desperate,
        which are as wind?
²⁷ Yea, ye overwhelm the fatherless,
    and ye dig a pit for your friend.
²⁸ Now therefore be content, look upon me;
    for it is evident unto you if I lie.
²⁹ Return, I pray you, let it not be iniquity;
    yea, return again, my righteousness is in it.
³⁰ Is there iniquity in my tongue?
    Cannot my taste discern perverse things?'

7   'Is there not an appointed time to man upon earth?
       Are not his days also like the days of an hireling?
[2] As a servant earnestly desireth the shadow, and as
       an hireling looketh for the reward of his work,
[3] so am I made to possess months of vanity,
       and wearisome nights are appointed to me.
[4] When I lie down, I say,
       "When shall I arise, and the night be gone?"
           and I am full of tossings to and fro
       unto the dawning of the day.
[5] My flesh is clothed with worms and clods of dust;
       my skin is broken, and become loathsome.
[6] My days are swifter than a weaver's shuttle,
       and are spent without hope.
[7] O remember that my life is wind:
       mine eye shall no more see good.
[8] The eye of him that hath seen me
       shall see me no more:
           thine eyes are upon me, and I am not.
[9] As the cloud is consumed and vanisheth away,
       so he that goeth down to the grave
           shall come up no more.
[10] He shall return no more to his house,
       neither shall his place know him any more.
[11] Therefore I will not refrain my mouth;
       I will speak in the anguish of my spirit;
           I will complain in the bitterness of my soul.

¹²Am I a sea, or a whale,
   that thou settest a watch over me?
¹³When I say, "My bed shall comfort me,
   my couch shall ease my complaint";
¹⁴then thou scarest me with dreams,
   and terrifiest me through visions;
¹⁵so that my soul chooseth strangling,
   and death rather than my life.
¹⁶I loathe it; I would not live alway.
   Let me alone; for my days are vanity.
¹⁷What is man, that thou shouldest magnify him?
   And that thou shouldest
       set thine heart upon him?
¹⁸And that thou shouldest visit him every morning,
   and try him every moment?
¹⁹How long wilt thou not depart from me,
   nor let me alone till I swallow down my spittle?
²⁰I have sinned; what shall I do unto thee,
   O thou preserver of men?
       Why hast thou set me as a mark against thee,
   so that I am a burden to myself?
²¹And why dost thou not pardon my transgression,
   and take away mine iniquity?
       For now shall I sleep in the dust;
   and thou shalt seek me in the morning,
       but I shall not be.'

8 Then answered Bildad the Shuhite, and said, [2] 'How long wilt thou speak these things? And how long shall the words of thy mouth be like a strong wind? [3] Doth God pervert judgement? Or doth the Almighty pervert justice? [4] If thy children have sinned against him, and he have cast them away for their transgression; [5] if thou wouldest seek unto God betimes, and make thy supplication to the Almighty; [6] if thou wert pure and upright; surely now he would awake for thee, and make the habitation of thy righteousness prosperous. [7] Though thy beginning was small, yet thy latter end should greatly increase. [8] For enquire, I pray thee, of the former age, and prepare thyself to the search of their fathers [9] (for we are but of yesterday, and know nothing, because our days upon earth are a shadow). [10] Shall not they teach thee, and tell thee, and utter words out of their heart? [11] Can the rush grow up without mire? Can the flag grow without water? [12] Whilst it is yet in his greenness, and not cut down, it withereth before any other herb. [13] So are the paths of all that forget God, and the hypocrite's hope shall perish; [14] whose hope shall be cut off, and whose trust shall be a spider's web. [15] He shall lean upon his house, but it shall not stand; he shall hold it fast, but it shall not endure. [16] He is green before the sun, and his branch shooteth forth in his garden. [17] His roots are wrapped about the heap, and seeth the place of stones. [18] If he destroy him from his place, then it shall deny him, saying, I have not seen thee. [19] Behold, this is the joy of his way, and out of the earth shall others grow. [20] Behold, God will not cast away a perfect man, neither will he help the evil doers; [21] till he fill

thy mouth with laughing, and thy lips with rejoicing. ²²They that hate thee shall be clothed with shame; and the dwelling place of the wicked shall come to nought.'

9 Then Job answered and said,

²'I know it is so of a truth;
    but how should man be just with God?
³If he will contend with him,
    he cannot answer him one of a thousand.
⁴He is wise in heart, and mighty in strength:
    who hath hardened himself against him,
        and hath prospered?
⁵Which removeth the mountains, and they know not;
    which overturneth them in his anger.
⁶Which shaketh the earth out of her place,
    and the pillars thereof tremble.
⁷Which commandeth the sun, and it riseth not;
    and sealeth up the stars.
⁸Which alone spreadeth out the heavens,
    and treadeth upon the waves of the sea.
⁹Which maketh Arcturus, Orion, and Pleiades,
    and the chambers of the south.
¹⁰Which doeth great things past finding out;
    yea, and wonders without number.
¹¹Lo, he goeth by me, and I see him not;
    he passeth on also, but I perceive him not.
¹²Behold, he taketh away, who can hinder him?

Who will say unto him, "What doest thou?"

¹³ If God will not withdraw his anger,
    the proud helpers do stoop under him.
¹⁴ How much less shall I answer him,
    and choose out my words to reason with him?
¹⁵ Whom, though I were righteous,
    yet would I not answer,
        but I would make supplication to my judge.
¹⁶ If I had called, and he had answered me;
    yet would I not believe that he had
        hearkened unto my voice.
¹⁷ For he breaketh me with a tempest,
    and multiplieth my wounds without cause.
¹⁸ He will not suffer me to take my breath,
    but filleth me with bitterness.
¹⁹ If I speak of strength, lo, he is strong; and,
    if of judgment, who shall set me a time to plead?
²⁰ If I justify myself, mine own mouth shall
    condemn me; if I say I am perfect,
        it shall also prove me perverse.
²¹ Though I were perfect,
    yet would I not know my soul:
        I would despise my life.
²² This is one thing, therefore I said it,
    He destroyeth the perfect and the wicked.
²³ If the scourge slay suddenly,
    he will laugh at the trial of the innocent.

²⁴ The earth is given into the hand of the wicked;
he covereth the faces of the judges thereof;
if not, where and who is he?
²⁵ Now my days are swifter than a post:
they flee away, they see no good.
²⁶ They are passed away as the swift ships;
as the eagle that hasteth to the prey.
²⁷ If I say, "I will forget my complaint,
I will leave off my heaviness,
and comfort myself,"
²⁸ I am afraid of all my sorrows,
I know that thou wilt not hold me innocent.
²⁹ If I be wicked, why then labour I in vain?
³⁰ If I wash myself with snow water,
and make my hands never so clean;
³¹ yet shalt thou plunge me in the ditch,
and mine own clothes shall abhor me.
³² For he is not a man, as I am,
that I should answer him,
and we should come together in judgment.
³³ Neither is there any daysman betwixt us,
that might lay his hand upon us both.
³⁴ Let him take his rod away from me,
and let not his fear terrify me;
³⁵ then would I speak, and not fear him;
but it is not so with me.'

10

'My soul is weary of my life;
   I will leave my complaint upon myself;
      I will speak in the bitterness of my soul.
² I will say unto God, "Do not condemn me;
   shew me wherefore thou contendest with me.
³ Is it good unto thee that thou shouldest oppress,
   that thou shouldest despise the work of thine hands,
      and shine upon the counsel of the wicked?
⁴ Hast thou eyes of flesh? Or seest thou as man seeth?
⁵ Are thy days as the days of man?
   Are thy years as man's days,
⁶ that thou enquirest after mine iniquity,
   and searchest after my sin?
⁷ Thou knowest that I am not wicked; and
   there is none that can deliver out of thine hand.
⁸ Thine hands have made me
   and fashioned me together round about;
      yet thou dost destroy me.
⁹ Remember, I beseech thee,
   that thou hast made me as the clay;
      and wilt thou bring me into dust again?
¹⁰ Hast thou not poured me out as milk,
   and curdled me like cheese?
¹¹ Thou hast clothed me with skin and flesh,
   and hast fenced me with bones and sinews.
¹² Thou hast granted me life and favour,
   and thy visitation hath preserved my spirit.
¹³ And these things hast thou hid in thine heart;

I know that this is with thee.
[14] If I sin, then thou markest me,
and thou wilt not acquit me from mine iniquity.
[15] If I be wicked, woe unto me;
and if I be righteous, yet will I not lift up my head.
I am full of confusion;
therefore see thou mine affliction,
[16] for it increaseth.
Thou huntest me as a fierce lion;
and again thou shewest thyself
marvellous upon me.
[17] Thou renewest thy witnesses against me,
and increasest thine indignation upon me;
changes and war are against me.
[18] "Wherefore then hast thou brought me forth
out of the womb?
Oh that I had given up the ghost,
and no eye had seen me!
[19] I should have been as though I had not been;
I should have been carried
from the womb to the grave.
[20] Are not my days few?
Cease then, and let me alone,
that I may take comfort a little,
[21] before I go whence I shall not return,
even to the land of darkness
and the shadow of death;
[22] a land of darkness, as darkness itself;

and of the shadow of death, without any order,
and where the light is as darkness."'

11 Then answered Zophar the Naamathite, and said,
² 'Should not the multitude of words be answered? And
should a man full of talk be justified? ³ Should thy lies make
men hold their peace? And when thou mockest, shall no man
make thee ashamed? ⁴ For thou hast said, "My doctrine is
pure, and I am clean in thine eyes." ⁵ But oh that God would
speak, and open his lips against thee; ⁶ and that he would
shew thee the secrets of wisdom, that they are double to that
which is! Know therefore that God exacteth of thee less than
thine iniquity deserveth. ⁷ Canst thou by searching find out
God? Canst thou find out the Almighty unto perfection? ⁸ It
is as high as heaven; what canst thou do? Deeper than hell;
what canst thou know? ⁹ The measure thereof is longer than
the earth, and broader than the sea. ¹⁰ If he cut off, and shut
up, or gather together, then who can hinder him? ¹¹ For he
knoweth vain men. He seeth wickedness also; will he not
then consider it? ¹² For vain man would be wise, though man
be born like a wild ass's colt. ¹³ If thou prepare thine heart,
and stretch out thine hands toward him; ¹⁴ if iniquity be in
thine hand, put it far away, and let not wickedness dwell in
thy tabernacles. ¹⁵ For then shalt thou lift up thy face without
spot; yea, thou shalt be stedfast, and shalt not fear, ¹⁶ because
thou shalt forget thy misery, and remember it as waters that
pass away. ¹⁷ And thine age shall be clearer than the noonday; thou shalt shine forth, thou shalt be as the morning.

¹⁸And thou shalt be secure, because there is hope; yea, thou shalt dig about thee, and thou shalt take thy rest in safety. ¹⁹Also thou shalt lie down, and none shall make thee afraid; yea, many shall make suit unto thee. ²⁰But the eyes of the wicked shall fail, and they shall not escape, and their hope shall be as the giving up of the ghost.'

12 And Job answered and said,

²'No doubt but ye are the people,
and wisdom shall die with you.
³But I have understanding as well as you;
I am not inferior to you:
yea, who knoweth not such things as these?
⁴I am as one mocked of his neighbour,
I who calleth upon God, and he answereth him:
the just upright man is laughed to scorn.
⁵He that is ready to slip with his feet
is as a lamp despised in the thought of him
that is at ease.
⁶The tabernacles of robbers prosper,
and they that provoke God are secure;
into whose hand God bringeth abundantly.
⁷But ask now the beasts, and they shall teach thee;
and the fowls of the air, and they shall tell thee.
⁸Or speak to the earth, and it shall teach thee;
and the fishes of the sea shall declare unto thee.
⁹Who knoweth not in all these that the hand of

the Lord hath wrought this?

¹⁰ In whose hand is the soul of every living thing,
and the breath of all mankind.

¹¹ Doth not the ear try words?
And the mouth taste his meat?

¹² With the ancient is wisdom;
and in length of days understanding.

¹³ With him is wisdom and strength,
he hath counsel and understanding.

¹⁴ Behold, he breaketh down,
and it cannot be built again;
he shutteth up a man,
and there can be no opening.

¹⁵ Behold, he withholdeth the waters, and they dry up;
also he sendeth them out,
and they overturn the earth.

¹⁶ With him is strength and wisdom;
the deceived and the deceiver are his.

¹⁷ He leadeth counsellors away spoiled,
and maketh the judges fools.

¹⁸ He looseth the bond of kings,
and girdeth their loins with a girdle.

¹⁹ He leadeth princes away spoiled,
and overthroweth the mighty.

²⁰ He removeth away the speech of the trusty,
and taketh away the understanding of the aged.

²¹ He poureth contempt upon princes,
and weakeneth the strength of the mighty.

²²He discovereth deep things out of darkness,
  and bringeth out to light the shadow of death.
²³He increaseth the nations, and destroyeth them;
  he enlargeth the nations,
    and straiteneth them again.
²⁴He taketh away the heart of the chief of
  the people of the earth,
    and causeth them to wander
  in a wilderness where there is no way.
²⁵They grope in the dark without light, and
  he maketh them to stagger like a drunken man.'

13 'Lo, mine eye hath seen all this,
  mine ear hath heard and understood it.
²What ye know, the same do I know also:
  I am not inferior unto you.
³Surely I would speak to the Almighty,
  and I desire to reason with God.
⁴But ye are forgers of lies,
  ye are all physicians of no value.
⁵O that ye would altogether hold your peace!
  And it should be your wisdom.
⁶Hear now my reasoning,
  and hearken to the pleadings of my lips.
⁷Will ye speak wickedly for God?
  And talk deceitfully for him?
⁸Will ye accept his person? Will ye contend for God?
⁹Is it good that he should search you out?

Or as one man mocketh another,
do ye so mock him?

¹⁰ He will surely reprove you,
if ye do secretly accept persons.

¹¹ Shall not his excellency make you afraid?
And his dread fall upon you?

¹² Your remembrances are like unto ashes,
your bodies to bodies of clay.

¹³ Hold your peace, let me alone, that I may speak,
and let come on me what will.

¹⁴ Wherefore do I take my flesh in my teeth,
and put my life in mine hand?

¹⁵ Though he slay me, yet will I trust in him;
but I will maintain mine own ways before him.

¹⁶ He also shall be my salvation;
for an hypocrite shall not come before him.

¹⁷ Hear diligently my speech,
and my declaration with your ears.

¹⁸ Behold now I have ordered my cause;
I know that I shall be justified.

¹⁹ Who is he that will plead with me?
For now, if I hold my tongue,
I shall give up the ghost.

²⁰ Only do not two things unto me;
then will I not hide myself from thee.

²¹ Withdraw thine hand far from me;
and let not thy dread make me afraid.

²² Then call thou, and I will answer;

or let me speak, and answer thou me.
23 How many are mine iniquities and sins?
    Make me to know my transgression and my sin.
24 Wherefore hidest thou thy face,
    and holdest me for thine enemy?
25 Wilt thou break a leaf driven to and fro?
    And wilt thou pursue the dry stubble?
26 For thou writest bitter things against me, and
    makest me to possess the iniquities of my youth.
27 Thou puttest my feet also in the stocks,
    and lookest narrowly unto all my paths;
        thou settest a print upon the heels of my feet.
28 And he, as a rotten thing, consumeth,
    as a garment that is moth eaten.'

14 'Man that is born of a woman is of few days,
    and full of trouble.
2 He cometh forth like a flower, and is cut down;
    he fleeth also as a shadow, and continueth not.
3 And dost thou open thine eyes upon such an one,
    and bringest me into judgment with thee?
4 Who can bring a clean thing out of an unclean?
    Not one.
5 Seeing his days are determined,
    the number of his months are with thee,
        and thou hast appointed his bounds
    that he cannot pass,
6 turn from him, that he may rest,

till he shall accomplish, as an hireling, his day.
⁷ For there is hope of a tree, if it be cut down,
    that it will sprout again, and
        that the tender branch thereof will not cease.
⁸ Though the root thereof wax old in the earth,
    and the stock thereof die in the ground,
⁹ yet through the scent of water it will bud,
    and bring forth boughs like a plant.
¹⁰ But man dieth, and wasteth away;
    yea, man giveth up the ghost, and where is he?
¹¹ As the waters fail from the sea,
    and the flood decayeth and drieth up,
¹² so man lieth down, and riseth not;
    till the heavens be no more, they shall not awake,
        nor be raised out of their sleep.
¹³ O that thou wouldest hide me in the grave,
    that thou wouldest keep me secret,
        until thy wrath be past, that thou wouldest
    appoint me a set time, and remember me!
¹⁴ If a man die, shall he live again?
    all the days of my appointed time will I wait,
        till my change come.
¹⁵ Thou shalt call, and I will answer thee:
    thou wilt have a desire to the work of thine hands.
¹⁶ For now thou numberest my steps;
    dost thou not watch over my sin?
¹⁷ My transgression is sealed up in a bag,
    and thou sewest up mine iniquity.

¹⁸And surely the mountain falling cometh to nought,
and the rock is removed out of his place.
¹⁹ The waters wear the stones;
thou washest away the things
which grow out of the dust of the earth;
and thou destroyest the hope of man.
²⁰ Thou prevailest for ever against him,
and he passeth; thou changest his countenance,
and sendest him away.
²¹ His sons come to honour, and he knoweth it not;
and they are brought low,
but he perceiveth it not of them.
²² But his flesh upon him shall have pain,
and his soul within him shall mourn.'

15 Then answered Eliphaz the Temanite, and said, ² 'Should a wise man utter vain knowledge, and fill his belly with the east wind? ³ Should he reason with unprofitable talk? Or with speeches wherewith he can do no good? ⁴ Yea, thou castest off fear, and restrainest prayer before God. ⁵ For thy mouth uttereth thine iniquity, and thou choosest the tongue of the crafty. ⁶ Thine own mouth condemneth thee, and not I; yea, thine own lips testify against thee. ⁷ Art thou the first man that was born? Or wast thou made before the hills? ⁸ Hast thou heard the secret of God? And dost thou restrain wisdom to thyself? ⁹ What knowest thou, that we know not? What understandest thou, which is not in us? ¹⁰ With us are both the grayheaded and very aged men, much elder than thy father. ¹¹ Are

the consolations of God small with thee? Is there any secret thing with thee? ¹² Why doth thine heart carry thee away? And what do thy eyes wink at, ¹³ that thou turnest thy spirit against God, and lettest such words go out of thy mouth? ¹⁴ What is man, that he should be clean? And he which is born of a woman, that he should be righteous? ¹⁵ Behold, he putteth no trust in his saints; yea, the heavens are not clean in his sight. ¹⁶ How much more abominable and filthy is man, which drinketh iniquity like water? ¹⁷ I will shew thee, hear me; and that which I have seen I will declare; ¹⁸ which wise men have told from their fathers, and have not hid it: ¹⁹ unto whom alone the earth was given, and no stranger passed among them. ²⁰ The wicked man travaileth with pain all his days, and the number of years is hidden to the oppressor. ²¹A dreadful sound is in his ears; in prosperity the destroyer shall come upon him. ²² He believeth not that he shall return out of darkness, and he is waited for of the sword. ²³ He wandereth abroad for bread, saying, "Where is it?" He knoweth that the day of darkness is ready at his hand. ²⁴ Trouble and anguish shall make him afraid; they shall prevail against him, as a king ready to the battle. ²⁵ For he stretcheth out his hand against God, and strengtheneth himself against the Almighty. ²⁶ He runneth upon him, even on his neck, upon the thick bosses of his bucklers; ²⁷ because he covereth his face with his fatness, and maketh collops of fat on his flanks. ²⁸And he dwelleth in desolate cities, and in houses which no man inhabiteth, which are ready to become heaps. ²⁹ He shall not be rich, neither shall his substance continue, neither shall he prolong the perfection thereof upon the earth. ³⁰ He shall not depart out of darkness; the flame shall dry up his branches, and by the breath of his mouth shall he go away. ³¹ Let not him that is deceived trust in vanity; for vanity shall be his recompence. ³² It shall be accomplished before his time, and his branch shall not be green. ³³ He shall shake off his unripe grape as the vine, and shall cast off his flower as the olive. ³⁴ For the congregation of hypocrites shall be desolate, and fire shall consume the tabernacles of bribery. ³⁵ They conceive mischief, and bring forth vanity, and their belly prepareth deceit.'

16 Then Job answered and said,

² 'I have heard many such things:
    miserable comforters are ye all.
³ Shall vain words have an end?
    Or what emboldeneth thee that thou answerest?
⁴ I also could speak as ye do;
    if your soul were in my soul's stead,
        I could heap up words against you,
    and shake mine head at you.
⁵ But I would strengthen you with my mouth, and
    the moving of my lips should assuage your grief.
⁶ Though I speak, my grief is not asswaged;
    and though I forbear, what am I eased?
⁷ But now he hath made me weary;
    thou hast made desolate all my company.
⁸ And thou hast filled me with wrinkles,

which is a witness against me; and my leanness
rising up in me beareth witness to my face.
⁹ He teareth me in his wrath, who hateth me;
he gnasheth upon me with his teeth;
mine enemy sharpeneth his eyes upon me.
¹⁰ They have gaped upon me with their mouth;
they have smitten me upon
the cheek reproachfully; they have gathered
themselves together against me.
¹¹ God hath delivered me to the ungodly,
and turned me over into the hands of the wicked.
¹² I was at ease, but he hath broken me asunder;
he hath also taken me by my neck, and shaken
me to pieces, and set me up for his mark.
¹³ His archers compass me round about,
he cleaveth my reins asunder, and doth not spare;
he poureth out my gall upon the ground.
¹⁴ He breaketh me with breach upon breach,
he runneth upon me like a giant.
¹⁵ I have sewed sackcloth upon my skin,
and defiled my horn in the dust.
¹⁶ My face is foul with weeping,
and on my eyelids is the shadow of death;
¹⁷ not for any injustice in mine hands,
also my prayer is pure.
¹⁸ O earth, cover not thou my blood,
and let my cry have no place.
¹⁹ Also now, behold, my witness is in heaven,

and my record is on high.
²⁰ My friends scorn me;
   but mine eye poureth out tears unto God.
²¹ O that one might plead for a man with God,
   as a man pleadeth for his neighbour!
²² When a few years are come,
   then I shall go the way whence I shall not return.'

17 'My breath is corrupt, my days are extinct,
   the graves are ready for me.
²Are there not mockers with me? And doth not
   mine eye continue in their provocation?
³ Lay down now, put me in a surety with thee;
   who is he that will strike hands with me?
⁴ For thou hast hid their heart from understanding;
   therefore shalt thou not exalt them.
⁵ He that speaketh flattery to his friends,
   even the eyes of his children shall fail.
⁶ He hath made me also a byword of the people;
   and aforetime I was as a tabret.
⁷ Mine eye also is dim by reason of sorrow,
   and all my members are as a shadow.
⁸ Upright men shall be astonied at this,
   and the innocent shall stir up himself
      against the hypocrite.
⁹ The righteous also shall hold on his way,
   and he that hath clean hands
      shall be stronger and stronger.

¹⁰ But as for you all, do ye return, and come now;
   for I cannot find one wise man among you.
¹¹ My days are past, my purposes are broken off,
   even the thoughts of my heart.
¹² They change the night into day;
   the light is short because of darkness.
¹³ If I wait, the grave is mine house;
   I have made my bed in the darkness.
¹⁴ I have said to corruption, "Thou art my father;"
   to the worm, "Thou art my mother, and my sister."
¹⁵ And where is now my hope?
   As for my hope, who shall see it?
¹⁶ They shall go down to the bars of the pit,
   when our rest together is in the dust.'

18 Then answered Bildad the Shuhite, and said, ² 'How long will it be ere ye make an end of words? Mark, and afterwards we will speak. ³ Wherefore are we counted as beasts, and reputed vile in your sight? ⁴ He teareth himself in his anger; shall the earth be forsaken for thee? And shall the rock be removed out of his place? ⁵ Yea, the light of the wicked shall be put out, and the spark of his fire shall not shine. ⁶ The light shall be dark in his tabernacle, and his candle shall be put out with him. ⁷ The steps of his strength shall be straitened, and his own counsel shall cast him down. ⁸ For he is cast into a net by his own feet, and he walketh upon a snare. ⁹ The gin shall take him by the heel, and the robber shall prevail against him. ¹⁰ The snare is laid for him in the ground,

and a trap for him in the way. ¹¹Terrors shall make him afraid on every side, and shall drive him to his feet. ¹²His strength shall be hungerbitten, and destruction shall be ready at his side. ¹³It shall devour the strength of his skin; even the first-born of death shall devour his strength. ¹⁴His confidence shall be rooted out of his tabernacle, and it shall bring him to the king of terrors. ¹⁵It shall dwell in his tabernacle, because it is none of his; brimstone shall be scattered upon his habitation. ¹⁶His roots shall be dried up beneath, and above shall his branch be cut off. ¹⁷His remembrance shall perish from the earth, and he shall have no name in the street. ¹⁸He shall be driven from light into darkness, and chased out of the world. ¹⁹He shall neither have son nor nephew among his people, nor any remaining in his dwellings. ²⁰They that come after him shall be astonied at his day, as they that went before were affrighted. ²¹Surely such are the dwellings of the wicked, and this is the place of him that knoweth not God.'

19 Then Job answered and said,

²'How long will ye vex my soul,
and break me in pieces with words?
³These ten times have ye reproached me;
ye are not ashamed that ye make
yourselves strange to me.
⁴And be it indeed that I have erred,
mine error remaineth with myself.
⁵If indeed ye will magnify yourselves against me,

and plead against me my reproach,

⁶ know now that God hath overthrown me,
and hath compassed me with his net.

⁷ Behold, I cry out of wrong, but I am not heard;
I cry aloud, but there is no judgment.

⁸ He hath fenced up my way that I cannot pass,
and he hath set darkness in my paths.

⁹ He hath stripped me of my glory,
and taken the crown from my head.

¹⁰ He hath destroyed me on every side,
and I am gone;
and mine hope hath he removed like a tree.

¹¹ He hath also kindled his wrath against me, and
he counteth me unto him as one of his enemies.

¹² His troops come together,
and raise up their way against me,
and encamp round about my tabernacle.

¹³ He hath put my brethren far from me, and
mine acquaintance are verily estranged from me.

¹⁴ My kinsfolk have failed,
and my familiar friends have forgotten me.

¹⁵ They that dwell in mine house,
and my maids, count me for a stranger:
I am an alien in their sight.

¹⁶ I called my servant, and he gave me no answer;
I intreated him with my mouth.

¹⁷ My breath is strange to my wife, though I intreated
for the children's sake of mine own body.

[18] Yea, young children despised me;
  I arose, and they spake against me.
[19] All my inward friends abhorred me:
  and they whom I loved are turned against me.
[20] My bone cleaveth to my skin and to my flesh,
  and I am escaped with the skin of my teeth.
[21] Have pity upon me, have pity upon me,
  O ye my friends;
    for the hand of God hath touched me.
[22] Why do ye persecute me as God,
  and are not satisfied with my flesh?
[23] 'Oh that my words were now written!
  Oh that they were printed in a book!
[24] That they were graven with an iron pen
  and lead in the rock for ever!
[25] For I know that my redeemer liveth, and that
  he shall stand at the latter day upon the earth;
[26] and though after my skin worms destroy this body,
  yet in my flesh shall I see God,
[27] whom I shall see for myself,
  and mine eyes shall behold, and not another,
    though my reins be consumed within me.
[28] But ye should say, "Why persecute we him,
  seeing the root of the matter is found in me?"
[29] Be ye afraid of the sword;
  for wrath bringeth the punishments of the sword,
    that ye may know there is a judgment.'

20 Then answered Zophar the Naamathite, and said, ² "Therefore do my thoughts cause me to answer, and for this I make haste. ³ I have heard the check of my reproach, and the spirit of my understanding causeth me to answer. ⁴ Knowest thou not this of old, since man was placed upon earth, ⁵ that the triumphing of the wicked is short, and the joy of the hypocrite but for a moment? ⁶ Though his excellency mount up to the heavens, and his head reach unto the clouds, ⁷ yet he shall perish for ever like his own dung; they which have seen him shall say, "Where is he?" ⁸ He shall fly away as a dream, and shall not be found; yea, he shall be chased away as a vision of the night. ⁹ The eye also which saw him shall see him no more; neither shall his place any more behold him. ¹⁰ His children shall seek to please the poor, and his hands shall restore their goods. ¹¹ His bones are full of the sin of his youth, which shall lie down with him in the dust. ¹² Though wickedness be sweet in his mouth, though he hide it under his tongue; ¹³ though he spare it, and forsake it not, but keep it still within his mouth; ¹⁴ yet his meat in his bowels is turned; it is the gall of asps within him. ¹⁵ He hath swallowed down riches, and he shall vomit them up again: God shall cast them out of his belly. ¹⁶ He shall suck the poison of asps: the viper's tongue shall slay him. ¹⁷ He shall not see the rivers, the floods, the brooks of honey and butter. ¹⁸ That which he laboured for shall he restore, and shall not swallow it down; according to his substance shall the restitution be, and he shall not rejoice therein. ¹⁹ Because he hath oppressed and hath forsaken the poor, because he hath violently taken away an house which he builded not, [20] surely he shall not feel quietness in his belly; he shall not save of that which he desired. [21] There shall none of his meat be left; therefore shall no man look for his goods. [22] In the fulness of his sufficiency he shall be in straits; every hand of the wicked shall come upon him. [23] When he is about to fill his belly, God shall cast the fury of his wrath upon him, and shall rain it upon him while he is eating. [24] He shall flee from the iron weapon, and the bow of steel shall strike him through. [25] It is drawn, and cometh out of the body; yea, the glittering sword cometh out of his gall: terrors are upon him. [26] All darkness shall be hid in his secret places; a fire not blown shall consume him; it shall go ill with him that is left in his tabernacle. [27] The heaven shall reveal his iniquity; and the earth shall rise up against him. [28] The increase of his house shall depart, and his goods shall flow away in the day of his wrath. [29] This is the portion of a wicked man from God, and the heritage appointed unto him by God.'

21 But Job answered and said,

[2] 'Hear diligently my speech,
    and let this be your consolations.
[3] Suffer me that I may speak;
    and after that I have spoken, mock on.
[4] As for me, is my complaint to man?
    And if it were so,
        why should not my spirit be troubled?
[5] Mark me, and be astonished,

and lay your hand upon your mouth.
⁶ Even when I remember I am afraid,
and trembling taketh hold on my flesh.
⁷ Wherefore do the wicked live, become old,
yea, are mighty in power?
⁸ Their seed is established in their sight with them,
and their offspring before their eyes.
⁹ Their houses are safe from fear;
neither is the rod of God upon them.
¹⁰ Their bull gendereth, and faileth not;
their cow calveth, and casteth not her calf.
¹¹ They send forth their little ones like a flock,
and their children dance.
¹² They take the timbrel and harp,
and rejoice at the sound of the organ.
¹³ They spend their days in wealth,
and in a moment go down to the grave.
¹⁴ Therefore they say unto God,
"Depart from us; for we desire not
the knowledge of thy ways.
¹⁵ What is the Almighty, that we should serve him?
And what profit should we have,
if we pray unto him?"
¹⁶ Lo, their good is not in their hand:
the counsel of the wicked is far from me.
¹⁷ How oft is the candle of the wicked put out!
And how oft cometh their destruction upon them!
God distributeth sorrows in his anger.

¹⁸ They are as stubble before the wind,
   and as chaff that the storm carrieth away.
¹⁹ God layeth up his iniquity for his children;
   he rewardeth him, and he shall know it.
²⁰ His eyes shall see his destruction,
   and he shall drink of the wrath of the Almighty.
²¹ For what pleasure hath he in his house after him,
   when the number of his months
      is cut off in the midst?
²² Shall any teach God knowledge,
   seeing he judgeth those that are high?
²³ One dieth in his full strength,
   being wholly at ease and quiet.
²⁴ His breasts are full of milk,
   and his bones are moistened with marrow.
²⁵ And another dieth in the bitterness of his soul,
   and never eateth with pleasure.
²⁶ They shall lie down alike in the dust,
   and the worms shall cover them.
²⁷ Behold, I know your thoughts,
   and the devices which ye wrongfully
      imagine against me.
²⁸ For ye say, "Where is the house of the prince?
   And where are the dwelling places of the wicked?"
²⁹ Have ye not asked them that go by the way?
   And do ye not know their tokens,
³⁰ that the wicked is reserved to the day of destruction?
   They shall be brought forth to the day of wrath.

³¹ Who shall declare his way to his face?
　　And who shall repay him what he hath done?
³² Yet shall he be brought to the grave,
　　and shall remain in the tomb.
³³ The clods of the valley shall be sweet unto him,
　　and every man shall draw after him,
　　　　as there are innumerable before him.
³⁴ How then comfort ye me in vain,
　　seeing in your answers
　　　　there remaineth falsehood?'

22 Then Eliphaz the Temanite answered and said, ² 'Can a man be profitable unto God, as he that is wise may be profitable unto himself? ³ Is it any pleasure to the Almighty, that thou art righteous? Or is it gain to him, that thou makest thy ways perfect? ⁴ Will he reprove thee for fear of thee? Will he enter with thee into judgment? ⁵ Is not thy wickedness great? And thine iniquities infinite? ⁶ For thou hast taken a pledge from thy brother for nought, and stripped the naked of their clothing. ⁷ Thou hast not given water to the weary to drink, and thou hast withholden bread from the hungry. ⁸ But as for the mighty man, he had the earth; and the honourable man dwelt in it. ⁹ Thou hast sent widows away empty, and the arms of the fatherless have been broken. ¹⁰ Therefore snares are round about thee, and sudden fear troubleth thee, ¹¹ Or darkness, that thou canst not see; and abundance of waters cover thee. ¹² Is not God in the height of heaven? And behold the height of the stars, how high they are! ¹³ And thou sayest, "How doth God know? Can he judge through the dark cloud?" ¹⁴ Thick clouds are a covering to him, that he seeth not; and he walketh in the circuit of heaven. ¹⁵ Hast thou marked the old way which wicked men have trodden? ¹⁶ Which were cut down out of time, whose foundation was overflown with a flood; ¹⁷ which said unto God, "Depart from us" and "What can the Almighty do for them?" ¹⁸ Yet he filled their houses with good things; but the counsel of the wicked is far from me. ¹⁹ The righteous see it, and are glad; and the innocent laugh them to scorn. ²⁰ Whereas our substance is not cut down, but the remnant of them the fire consumeth. ²¹ Acquaint now thyself with him, and be at peace; thereby good shall come unto thee. ²² Receive, I pray thee, the law from his mouth, and lay up his words in thine heart. ²³ If thou return to the Almighty, thou shalt be built up; thou shalt put away iniquity far from thy tabernacles. ²⁴ Then shalt thou lay up gold as dust, and the gold of Ophir as the stones of the brooks. ²⁵ Yea, the Almighty shall be thy defence, and thou shalt have plenty of silver. ²⁶ For then shalt thou have thy delight in the Almighty, and shalt lift up thy face unto God. ²⁷ Thou shalt make thy prayer unto him, and he shall hear thee, and thou shalt pay thy vows. ²⁸ Thou shalt also decree a thing, and it shall be established unto thee; and the light shall shine upon thy ways. ²⁹ When men are cast down, then thou shalt say, "There is lifting up"; and he shall save the humble person. ³⁰ He shall deliver the island of the innocent; and it is delivered by the pureness of thine hands.'

23 Then Job answered and said,

² 'Even to day is my complaint bitter;
  my stroke is heavier than my groaning.
³ Oh that I knew where I might find him!
  That I might come even to his seat!
⁴ I would order my cause before him,
  and fill my mouth with arguments.
⁵ I would know the words which he would answer me,
  and understand what he would say unto me.
⁶ Will he plead against me with his great power?
  No, but he would put strength in me.
⁷ There the righteous might dispute with him;
  so should I be delivered for ever from my judge.
⁸ Behold, I go forward, but he is not there;
  and backward, but I cannot perceive him;
⁹ on the left hand, where he doth work,
  but I cannot behold him;
    he hideth himself on the right hand,
  that I cannot see him.
¹⁰ But he knoweth the way that I take;
  when he hath tried me, I shall come forth as gold.
¹¹ My foot hath held his steps;
  his way have I kept, and not declined.
¹² Neither have I gone back from
  the commandment of his lips;
    I have esteemed the words of his mouth
  more than my necessary food.

¹³ But he is in one mind, and who can turn him?
  And what his soul desireth, even that he doeth.
¹⁴ For he performeth the thing that is appointed for me;
  and many such things are with him.
¹⁵ Therefore am I troubled at his presence;
  when I consider, I am afraid of him.
¹⁶ For God maketh my heart soft,
  and the Almighty troubleth me,
¹⁷ Because I was not cut off before the darkness,
  neither hath he covered the darkness from my face.'

24 'Why, seeing times are not hidden from the Almighty,
  do they that know him not see his days?
² Some remove the landmarks;
  they violently take away flocks, and feed thereof.
³ They drive away the ass of the fatherless,
  they take the widow's ox for a pledge.
⁴ They turn the needy out of the way;
  the poor of the earth hide themselves together.
⁵ Behold, as wild asses in the desert,
  go they forth to their work,
    rising betimes for a prey;
  the wilderness yieldeth food for them
    and for their children.
⁶ They reap every one his corn in the field;
  and they gather the vintage of the wicked.
⁷ They cause the naked to lodge without clothing,
  that they have no covering in the cold.

⁸ They are wet with the showers of the mountains,
  and embrace the rock for want of a shelter.
⁹ They pluck the fatherless from the breast,
  and take a pledge of the poor.
¹⁰ They cause him to go naked without clothing,
  and they take away the sheaf from the hungry;
¹¹ which make oil within their walls,
  and tread their winepresses, and suffer thirst.
¹² Men groan from out of the city,
  and the soul of the wounded crieth out;
    yet God layeth not folly to them.
¹³ They are of those that rebel against the light;
  they know not the ways thereof,
    nor abide in the paths thereof.
¹⁴ The murderer rising with the light killeth the poor
  and needy, and in the night is as a thief.
¹⁵ The eye also of the adulterer waiteth for
  the twilight, saying, "No eye shall see me;"
    and disguiseth his face.
¹⁶ In the dark they dig through houses,
  which they had marked for themselves
    in the daytime;
  they know not the light.
¹⁷ For the morning is to them
  even as the shadow of death;
    if one know them,
  they are in the terrors of the shadow of death.
¹⁸ He is swift as the waters;

their portion is cursed in the earth;
> he beholdeth not the way of the vineyards.

¹⁹ Drought and heat consume the snow waters;
> so doth the grave those which have sinned.

²⁰ The womb shall forget him;
> the worm shall feed sweetly on him;
>> he shall be no more remembered;
> and wickedness shall be broken as a tree.

²¹ He evil entreateth the barren that beareth not;
> and doeth not good to the widow.

²² He draweth also the mighty with his power;
> he riseth up, and no man is sure of life.

²³ Though it be given him to be in safety,
> whereon he resteth;
>> yet his eyes are upon their ways.

²⁴ They are exalted for a little while,
> but are gone and brought low;
>> they are taken out of the way as all other,
> and cut off as the tops of the ears of corn.

²⁵ And if it be not so now, who will make me a liar,
> and make my speech nothing worth?'

25 Then answered Bildad the Shuhite, and said, ² 'Dominion and fear are with him, he maketh peace in his high places. ³ Is there any number of his armies? And upon whom doth not his light arise? ⁴ How then can man be justified with God? Or how can he be clean that is born of a woman? ⁵ Behold even to the moon, and it shineth not; yea,

the stars are not pure in his sight. ⁶How much less man, that
is a worm? And the son of man, which is a worm?'

26 But Job answered and said,

²'How hast thou helped him that is without power?
   How savest thou the arm that hath no strength?
³How hast thou counselled him that hath no wisdom?
      And how hast thou plentifully declared
      the thing as it is?
⁴To whom hast thou uttered words?
   And whose spirit came from thee?
⁵Dead things are formed from under the waters,
   and the inhabitants thereof.
⁶Hell is naked before him,
   and destruction hath no covering.
⁷He stretcheth out the north over the empty place,
   and hangeth the earth upon nothing.
⁸He bindeth up the waters in his thick clouds;
   and the cloud is not rent under them.
⁹He holdeth back the face of his throne,
   and spreadeth his cloud upon it.
¹⁰He hath compassed the waters with bounds,
   until the day and night come to an end.
¹¹The pillars of heaven tremble
   and are astonished at his reproof.
¹²He divideth the sea with his power, and by his
   understanding he smiteth through the proud.

¹³ By his spirit he hath garnished the heavens;
   his hand hath formed the crooked serpent.
¹⁴ Lo, these are parts of his ways;
   but how little a portion is heard of him?
      But the thunder of his power
   who can understand?'

27 Moreover Job continued his parable, and said,

² 'As God liveth, who hath taken away my judgment,
   and the Almighty, who hath vexed my soul,
³ all the while my breath is in me,
   and the spirit of God is in my nostrils,
⁴ my lips shall not speak wickedness,
   nor my tongue utter deceit.
⁵ God forbid that I should justify you;
   till I die I will not remove mine integrity from me.
⁶ My righteousness I hold fast, and will not let it go;
   my heart shall not reproach me so long as I live.
⁷ Let mine enemy be as the wicked, and
   he that riseth up against me as the unrighteous.
⁸ For what is the hope of the hypocrite,
   though he hath gained,
      when God taketh away his soul?
⁹ Will God hear his cry when trouble
   cometh upon him?
¹⁰ Will he delight himself in the Almighty?
   Will he always call upon God?

¹¹ I will teach you by the hand of God;
that which is with the Almighty will I not conceal.
¹² Behold, all ye yourselves have seen it;
why then are ye thus altogether vain?
¹³ This is the portion of a wicked man with God,
and the heritage of oppressors,
which they shall receive of the Almighty.
¹⁴ If his children be multiplied, it is for the sword;
and his offspring shall not be satisfied with bread.
¹⁵ Those that remain of him shall be buried in death;
and his widows shall not weep.
¹⁶ Though he heap up silver as the dust,
and prepare raiment as the clay,
¹⁷ he may prepare it, but the just shall put it on,
and the innocent shall divide the silver.
¹⁸ He buildeth his house as a moth,
and as a booth that the keeper maketh.
¹⁹ The rich man shall lie down,
but he shall not be gathered;
he openeth his eyes, and he is not.
²⁰ Terrors take hold on him as waters,
a tempest stealeth him away in the night.
²¹ The east wind carrieth him away, and he departeth;
and as a storm hurleth him out of his place.
²² For God shall cast upon him, and not spare;
he would fain flee out of his hand.
²³ Men shall clap their hands at him,
and shall hiss him out of his place.'

28

'Surely there is a vein for the silver,
 and a place for gold where they fine it.
² Iron is taken out of the earth,
 and brass is molten out of the stone.
³ He setteth an end to darkness,
 and searcheth out all perfection;
 the stones of darkness, and the shadow of death.
⁴ The flood breaketh out from the inhabitant,
 even the waters forgotten of the foot;
 they are dried up,
 they are gone away from men.
⁵ As for the earth, out of it cometh bread;
 and under it is turned up as it were fire.
⁶ The stones of it are the place of sapphires;
 and it hath dust of gold.
⁷ There is a path which no fowl knoweth,
 and which the vulture's eye hath not seen;
⁸ the lion's whelps have not trodden it,
 nor the fierce lion passed by it.
⁹ He putteth forth his hand upon the rock;
 he overturneth the mountains by the roots.
¹⁰ He cutteth out rivers among the rocks;
 and his eye seeth every precious thing.
¹¹ He bindeth the floods from overflowing;
 and the thing that is hid bringeth he forth to light.
¹² But where shall wisdom be found?
 And where is the place of understanding?
¹³ Man knoweth not the price thereof;

neither is it found in the land of the living.

¹⁴ The depth saith, "It is not in me;"

and the sea saith, "It is not with me."

¹⁵ It cannot be gotten for gold, neither shall silver

be weighed for the price thereof.

¹⁶ It cannot be valued with the gold of Ophir,

with the precious onyx, or the sapphire.

¹⁷ The gold and the crystal cannot equal it;

and the exchange of it

shall not be for jewels of fine gold.

¹⁸ No mention shall be made of coral, or of pearls,

for the price of wisdom is above rubies.

¹⁹ The topaz of Ethiopia shall not equal it,

neither shall it be valued with pure gold.

²⁰ Whence then cometh wisdom?

And where is the place of understanding,

²¹ seeing it is hid from the eyes of all living,

and kept close from the fowls of the air?

²² Destruction and death say,

"We have heard the fame thereof with our ears."

²³ God understandeth the way thereof,

and he knoweth the place thereof.

²⁴ For he looketh to the ends of the earth,

and seeth under the whole heaven,

²⁵ to make the weight for the winds;

and he weigheth the waters by measure.

²⁶ When he made a decree for the rain,

and a way for the lightning of the thunder,

²⁷then did he see it, and declare it;
   he prepared it, yea, and searched it out.
²⁸And unto man he said,
   "Behold, the fear of the Lord, that is wisdom;
      and to depart from evil is understanding."'

29

Moreover Job continued his parable, and said,

² 'Oh that I were as in months past,
   as in the days when God preserved me;
³ when his candle shined upon my head,
   and when by his light I walked through darkness,
⁴ as I was in the days of my youth,
   when the secret of God was upon my tabernacle;
⁵ when the Almighty was yet with me,
   when my children were about me;
⁶ when I washed my steps with butter,
   and the rock poured me out rivers of oil;
⁷ when I went out to the gate through the city,
   when I prepared my seat in the street,
⁸ the young men saw me, and hid themselves;
   and the aged arose, and stood up.
⁹ The princes refrained talking,
   and laid their hand on their mouth.
¹⁰ The nobles held their peace, and their tongue
   cleaved to the roof of their mouth.
¹¹ When the ear heard me, then it blessed me;
   and when the eye saw me, it gave witness to me;

¹²because I delivered the poor that cried, and
the fatherless, and him that had none to help him.
¹³The blessing of him that was ready to perish
came upon me;
and I caused the widow's heart to sing for joy.
¹⁴I put on righteousness, and it clothed me;
my judgment was as a robe and a diadem.
¹⁵I was eyes to the blind, and feet was I to the lame.
¹⁶I was a father to the poor;
and the cause which I knew not I searched out.
¹⁷And I brake the jaws of the wicked,
and plucked the spoil out of his teeth.
¹⁸Then I said, "I shall die in my nest,
and I shall multiply my days as the sand."
¹⁹My root was spread out by the waters,
and the dew lay all night upon my branch.
²⁰My glory was fresh in me,
and my bow was renewed in my hand.
²¹Unto me men gave ear, and waited,
and kept silence at my counsel.
²²After my words they spake not again;
and my speech dropped upon them.
²³And they waited for me as for the rain;
and they opened their mouth wide
as for the latter rain.
²⁴If I laughed on them, they believed it not;
and the light of my countenance
they cast not down.

²⁵ I chose out their way, and sat chief,
    and dwelt as a king in the army,
        as one that comforteth the mourners.'

30 'But now they that are younger than I
    have me in derision,
        whose fathers I would have disdained
    to have set with the dogs of my flock.
² Yea, whereto might the strength of their hands
    profit me, in whom old age was perished?
³ For want and famine they were solitary;
    fleeing into the wilderness in former time
        desolate and waste;
⁴ who cut up mallows by the bushes,
    and juniper roots for their meat.
⁵ They were driven forth from among men
    (they cried after them as after a thief)
⁶ to dwell in the clifts of the valleys,
    in caves of the earth, and in the rocks.
⁷ Among the bushes they brayed;
    under the nettles they were gathered together.
⁸ They were children of fools,
    yea, children of base men;
        they were viler than the earth.
⁹ And now am I their song, yea, I am their byword.
¹⁰ They abhor me, they flee far from me,
    and spare not to spit in my face.
¹¹ Because he hath loosed my cord, and afflicted me,

they have also let loose the bridle before me.

¹² Upon my right hand rise the youth;
   they push away my feet,
      and they raise up against me
   the ways of their destruction.

¹³ They mar my path, they set forward my calamity,
   they have no helper.

¹⁴ They came upon me as a wide breaking in of waters;
   in the desolation they rolled themselves upon me.

¹⁵ Terrors are turned upon me;
   they pursue my soul as the wind;
      and my welfare passeth away as a cloud.

¹⁶ And now my soul is poured out upon me;
   the days of affliction have taken hold upon me.

¹⁷ My bones are pierced in me in the night season;
   and my sinews take no rest.

¹⁸ By the great force of my disease
   is my garment changed;
      it bindeth me about as the collar of my coat.

¹⁹ He hath cast me into the mire,
   and I am become like dust and ashes.

²⁰ I cry unto thee, and thou dost not hear me:
   I stand up, and thou regardest me not.

²¹ Thou art become cruel to me;
   with thy strong hand
      thou opposest thyself against me.

²² Thou liftest me up to the wind;
   thou causest me to ride upon it,

and dissolvest my substance.
²³ For I know that thou wilt bring me to death,
and to the house appointed for all living.
²⁴ Howbeit he will not stretch out
his hand to the grave,
though they cry in his destruction.
²⁵ Did not I weep for him that was in trouble?
Was not my soul grieved for the poor?
²⁶ When I looked for good, then evil came unto me;
and when I waited for light, there came darkness.
²⁷ My bowels boiled, and rested not;
the days of affliction prevented me.
²⁸ I went mourning without the sun;
I stood up, and I cried in the congregation.
²⁹ I am a brother to dragons,
and a companion to owls.
³⁰ My skin is black upon me,
and my bones are burned with heat.
³¹ My harp also is turned to mourning,
and my organ into the voice of them that weep.'

31 'I made a covenant with mine eyes;
why then should I think upon a maid?
² For what portion of God is there from above?
And what inheritance
of the Almighty from on high?
³ Is not destruction to the wicked?
And a strange punishment

to the workers of iniquity?

⁴Doth not he see my ways, and count all my steps?

⁵If I have walked with vanity,

or if my foot hath hasted to deceit,

⁶let me be weighed in an even balance,

that God may know mine integrity.

⁷If my step hath turned out of the way,

and mine heart walked after mine eyes,

and if any blot hath cleaved to mine hands,

⁸then let me sow, and let another eat;

yea, let my offspring be rooted out.

⁹If mine heart have been deceived by a woman,

or if I have laid wait at my neighbour's door,

¹⁰then let my wife grind unto another,

and let others bow down upon her.

¹¹For this is an heinous crime;

yea, it is an iniquity to be punished by the judges.

¹²For it is a fire that consumeth to destruction,

and would root out all mine increase.

¹³If I did despise the cause of my manservant

or of my maidservant,

when they contended with me,

¹⁴what then shall I do when God riseth up?

And when he visiteth, what shall I answer him?

¹⁵Did not he that made me in the womb make him?

And did not one fashion us in the womb?

¹⁶If I have withheld the poor from their desire,

or have caused the eyes of the widow to fail;

¹⁷or have eaten my morsel myself alone,
and the fatherless hath not eaten thereof
¹⁸(for from my youth he was brought up with me,
as with a father,
and I have guided her
from my mother's womb);
¹⁹if I have seen any perish for want of clothing,
or any poor without covering;
²⁰if his loins have not blessed me,
and if he were not warmed
with the fleece of my sheep;
²¹if I have lifted up my hand against the fatherless,
when I saw my help in the gate:
²²then let mine arm fall from my shoulder blade,
and mine arm be broken from the bone.
²³For destruction from God was a terror to me,
and by reason of his highness I could not endure.
²⁴If I have made gold my hope,
or have said to the fine gold,
"Thou art my confidence;"
²⁵if I rejoiced because my wealth was great,
and because mine hand had gotten much;
²⁶if I beheld the sun when it shined,
or the moon walking in brightness;
²⁷and my heart hath been secretly enticed,
or my mouth hath kissed my hand:
²⁸this also were an iniquity
to be punished by the judge;

for I should have denied the God that is above.
²⁹ If I rejoiced at the destruction of him that hated me,
   or lifted up myself when evil found him,
³⁰ neither have I suffered my mouth to sin
   by wishing a curse to his soul.
³¹ If the men of my tabernacle said not,
   "Oh that we had of his flesh!"
      we cannot be satisfied.
³² The stranger did not lodge in the street;
   but I opened my doors to the traveller.
³³ If I covered my transgressions as Adam,
   by hiding mine iniquity in my bosom,
³⁴ did I fear a great multitude,
   or did the contempt of families terrify me,
      that I kept silence,
   and went not out of the door?
³⁵ Oh that one would hear me!
   Behold, my desire is that the Almighty
      would answer me,
   and that mine adversary had written a book.
³⁶ Surely I would take it upon my shoulder,
   and bind it as a crown to me.
³⁷ I would declare unto him the number of my steps;
   as a prince would I go near unto him.
³⁸ If my land cry against me,
   or that the furrows likewise thereof complain;
³⁹ if I have eaten the fruits thereof without money,
   or have caused the owners thereof to lose their life,

⁴⁰ let thistles grow instead of wheat,
and cockle instead of barley.'

The words of Job are ended.

32 So these three men ceased to answer Job, because he was righteous in his own eyes. ² Then was kindled the wrath of Elihu the son of Barachel the Buzite, of the kindred of Ram; against Job was his wrath kindled, because he justified himself rather than God. ³ Also against his three friends was his wrath kindled, because they had found no answer, and yet had condemned Job. ⁴ Now Elihu had waited till Job had spoken, because they were elder than he. ⁵ When Elihu saw that there was no answer in the mouth of these three men, then his wrath was kindled. ⁶ And Elihu the son of Barachel the Buzite answered and said,

'I am young, and ye are very old; wherefore I was afraid, and durst not shew you mine opinion. ⁷ I said, "Days should speak, and multitude of years should teach wisdom."⁸ But there is a spirit in man; and the inspiration of the Almighty giveth them understanding. ⁹ Great men are not always wise; neither do the aged understand judgment. ¹⁰ Therefore I said, "Hearken to me; I also will shew mine opinion."

¹¹ 'Behold, I waited for your words; I gave ear to your reasons, whilst ye searched out what to say. ¹² Yea, I attended unto you, and, behold, there was none of you that convinced Job, or that answered his words: ¹³ lest ye should say, "We have found out wisdom: God thrusteth him down, not man."

[14] Now he hath not directed his words against me; neither will I answer him with your speeches.

[15] 'They were amazed, they answered no more; they left off speaking. [16] When I had waited (for they spake not, but stood still, and answered no more), [17] I said, "I will answer also my part, I also will shew mine opinion." [18] For I am full of matter; the spirit within me constraineth me. [19] Behold, my belly is as wine which hath no vent; it is ready to burst like new bottles. [20] I will speak, that I may be refreshed; I will open my lips and answer. [21] Let me not, I pray you, accept any man's person, neither let me give flattering titles unto man. [22] For I know not to give flattering titles; in so doing my maker would soon take me away.

33 'Wherefore, Job, I pray thee, hear my speeches, and hearken to all my words. [2] Behold, now I have opened my mouth, my tongue hath spoken in my mouth. [3] My words shall be of the uprightness of my heart; and my lips shall utter knowledge clearly. [4] The Spirit of God hath made me, and the breath of the Almighty hath given me life. [5] If thou canst answer me, set thy words in order before me, stand up. [6] Behold, I am according to thy wish in God's stead; I also am formed out of the clay. [7] Behold, my terror shall not make thee afraid, neither shall my hand be heavy upon thee.

[8] 'Surely thou hast spoken in mine hearing, and I have heard the voice of thy words, saying, [9] "I am clean without transgression, I am innocent; neither is there iniquity in me." [10] Behold, he findeth occasions against me, he counteth me

for his enemy, [11]he putteth my feet in the stocks, he marketh all my paths.

[12]'Behold, in this thou art not just; I will answer thee, that God is greater than man. [13]Why dost thou strive against him? For he giveth not account of any of his matters. [14]For God speaketh once, yea twice, yet man perceiveth it not. [15]In a dream, in a vision of the night, when deep sleep falleth upon men, in slumberings upon the bed; [16]then he openeth the ears of men, and sealeth their instruction, [17]that he may withdraw man from his purpose, and hide pride from man. [18]He keepeth back his soul from the pit, and his life from perishing by the sword. [19]He is chastened also with pain upon his bed, and the multitude of his bones with strong pain; [20]so that his life abhorreth bread, and his soul dainty meat. [21]His flesh is consumed away, that it cannot be seen; and his bones that were not seen stick out. [22]Yea, his soul draweth near unto the grave, and his life to the destroyers. [23]If there be a messenger with him, an interpreter, one among a thousand, to shew unto man his uprightness; [24]then he is gracious unto him, and saith, "Deliver him from going down to the pit; I have found a ransom. [25]His flesh shall be fresher than a child's: he shall return to the days of his youth." [26]He shall pray unto God, and he will be favour-able unto him, and he shall see his face with joy; for he will render unto man his righteousness. [27]He looketh upon men, and if any say, "I have sinned, and perverted that which was right, and it profited me not;" [28]he will deliver his soul from going into the pit, and his life shall see the light.

²⁹ 'Lo, all these things worketh God oftentimes with man, ³⁰ to bring back his soul from the pit, to be enlightened with the light of the living. ³¹ Mark well, O Job, hearken unto me: hold thy peace, and I will speak. ³² If thou hast any thing to say, answer me; speak, for I desire to justify thee. ³³ If not, hearken unto me: hold thy peace, and I shall teach thee wisdom.'

34

Furthermore Elihu answered and said, ² 'Hear my words, O ye wise men; and give ear unto me, ye that have knowledge. ³ For the ear trieth words, as the mouth tasteth meat. ⁴ Let us choose to us judgment; let us know among ourselves what is good. ⁵ For Job hath said, I am righteous; and God hath taken away my judgment. ⁶ Should I lie against my right? My wound is incurable without transgression. ⁷ What man is like Job, who drinketh up scorning like water, ⁸ which goeth in company with the workers of iniquity, and walketh with wicked men? ⁹ For he hath said, "It profiteth a man nothing that he should delight himself with God." ¹⁰ 'Therefore hearken unto me, ye men of understanding: far be it from God, that he should do wickedness; and from the Almighty, that he should commit iniquity. ¹¹ For the work of a man shall he render unto him, and cause every man to find according to his ways. ¹² Yea, surely God will not do wickedly, neither will the Almighty pervert judgment. ¹³ Who hath given him a charge over the earth? Or who hath disposed the whole world? ¹⁴ If he set his heart upon man, if he gather unto himself his spirit and his breath, ¹⁵ all flesh shall perish together, and man shall turn again unto dust.

¹⁶ 'If now thou hast understanding, hear this: hearken to the voice of my words. ¹⁷ Shall even he that hateth right govern? And wilt thou condemn him that is most just? ¹⁸ Is it fit to say to a king, "Thou art wicked?" and to princes, "Ye are ungodly"? ¹⁹ How much less to him that accepteth not the persons of princes, nor regardeth the rich more than the poor? For they all are the work of his hands. ²⁰ In a moment shall they die, and the people shall be troubled at midnight, and pass away; and the mighty shall be taken away without hand.

²¹ 'For his eyes are upon the ways of man, and he seeth all his goings. ²² There is no darkness, nor shadow of death, where the workers of iniquity may hide themselves. ²³ For he will not lay upon man more than right; that he should enter into judgment with God. ²⁴ He shall break in pieces mighty men without number, and set others in their stead. ²⁵ Therefore he knoweth their works, and he overturneth them in the night, so that they are destroyed. ²⁶ He striketh them as wicked men in the open sight of others, ²⁷ because they turned back from him, and would not consider any of his ways, ²⁸ so that they cause the cry of the poor to come unto him, and he heareth the cry of the afflicted. ²⁹ When he giveth quietness, who then can make trouble? And when he hideth his face, who then can behold him? Whether it be done against a nation, or against a man only: ³⁰ that the hypocrite reign not, lest the people be ensnared.

³¹ 'Surely it is meet to be said unto God, "I have borne chastisement, I will not offend any more; ³² that which I see not teach thou me. If I have done iniquity, I will do no more."

³³ Should it be according to thy mind? He will recompense it, whether thou refuse, or whether thou choose; and not I. Therefore speak what thou knowest. ³⁴ Let men of understanding tell me, and let a wise man hearken unto me. ³⁵ Job hath spoken without knowledge, and his words were without wisdom. ³⁶ My desire is that Job may be tried unto the end because of his answers for wicked men. ³⁷ For he addeth rebellion unto his sin, he clappeth his hands among us, and multiplieth his words against God.'

35

Elihu spake moreover, and said, ² 'Thinkest thou this to be right, that thou saidst, "My righteousness is more than God's"? ³ For thou saidst, "What advantage will it be unto thee?" and "What profit shall I have, if I be cleansed from my sin?" ⁴ I will answer thee, and thy companions with thee. ⁵ Look unto the heavens, and see; and behold the clouds which are higher than thou. ⁶ If thou sinnest, what doest thou against him? Or if thy transgressions be multiplied, what doest thou unto him? ⁷ If thou be righteous, what givest thou him? Or what receiveth he of thine hand? ⁸ Thy wickedness may hurt a man as thou art; and thy righteousness may profit the son of man.

⁹ 'By reason of the multitude of oppressions they make the oppressed to cry; they cry out by reason of the arm of the mighty. ¹⁰ But none saith, "Where is God my maker, who giveth songs in the night; ¹¹ who teacheth us more than the beasts of the earth, and maketh us wiser than the fowls of heaven?" ¹² There they cry, but none giveth answer, because

of the pride of evil men. ¹³ Surely God will not hear vanity, neither will the Almighty regard it. ¹⁴ Although thou sayest thou shalt not see him, yet judgment is before him; therefore trust thou in him. ¹⁵ But now, because it is not so, he hath visited in his anger; yet he knoweth it not in great extremity. ¹⁶ Therefore doth Job open his mouth in vain; he multiplieth words without knowledge.'

36 Elihu also proceeded, and said, ² 'Suffer me a little, and I will shew thee that I have yet to speak on God's behalf. ³ I will fetch my knowledge from afar, and will ascribe righteousness to my Maker. ⁴ For truly my words shall not be false; he that is perfect in knowledge is with thee.

⁵ 'Behold, God is mighty, and despiseth not any; he is mighty in strength and wisdom. ⁶ He preserveth not the life of the wicked, but giveth right to the poor. ⁷ He withdraweth not his eyes from the righteous; but with kings are they on the throne; yea, he doth establish them for ever, and they are exalted. ⁸ And if they be bound in fetters, and be holden in cords of affliction; ⁹ then he sheweth them their work, and their transgressions that they have exceeded. ¹⁰ He openeth also their ear to discipline, and commandeth that they return from iniquity. ¹¹ If they obey and serve him, they shall spend their days in prosperity, and their years in pleasures. ¹² But if they obey not, they shall perish by the sword, and they shall die without knowledge. ¹³ 'But the hypocrites in heart heap up wrath: they cry not when he bindeth them. ¹⁴ They die in youth, and their life is among the unclean. ¹⁵ He delivereth

the poor in his affliction, and openeth their ears in oppression. [16] Even so would he have removed thee out of the strait into a broad place, where there is no straitness; and that which should be set on thy table should be full of fatness.

[17] 'But thou hast fulfilled the judgment of the wicked; judgment and justice take hold on thee. [18] Because there is wrath, beware lest he take thee away with his stroke; then a great ransom cannot deliver thee. [19] Will he esteem thy riches? No, not gold, nor all the forces of strength. [20] Desire not the night, when people are cut off in their place. [21] Take heed, regard not iniquity; for this hast thou chosen rather than affliction. [22] Behold, God exalteth by his power; who teacheth like him? [23] Who hath enjoined him his way? Or who can say, "Thou hast wrought iniquity"?

[24] 'Remember that thou magnify his work, which men behold. [25] Every man may see it; man may behold it afar off. [26] Behold, God is great, and we know him not, neither can the number of his years be searched out. [27] For he maketh small the drops of water; they pour down rain according to the vapour thereof, [28] which the clouds do drop and distil upon man abundantly. [29] Also can any understand the spreadings of the clouds, or the noise of his tabernacle? [30] Behold, he spreadeth his light upon it, and covereth the bottom of the sea. [31] For by them judgeth he the people; he giveth meat in abundance. [32] With clouds he covereth the light; and commandeth it not to shine by the cloud that cometh betwixt. [33] The noise thereof sheweth concerning it, the cattle also concerning the vapour.

37 'At this also my heart trembleth, and is moved out of his place. ² Hear attentively the noise of his voice, and the sound that goeth out of his mouth. ³ He directeth it under the whole heaven, and his lightning unto the ends of the earth. ⁴After it a voice roareth; he thundereth with the voice of his excellency; and he will not stay them when his voice is heard. ⁵ God thundereth marvellously with his voice; great things doeth he, which we cannot comprehend. ⁶ For he saith to the snow, "Be thou on the earth;" likewise to the small rain, and to the great rain of his strength. ⁷ He sealeth up the hand of every man; that all men may know his work. ⁸ Then the beasts go into dens, and remain in their places. ⁹Out of the south cometh the whirlwind; and cold out of the north. ¹⁰ By the breath of God frost is given; and the breadth of the waters is straitened. ¹¹Also by watering he wearieth the thick cloud, he scattereth his bright cloud; ¹² and it is turned round about by his counsels, that they may do whatsoever he commandeth them upon the face of the world in the earth. ¹³ He causeth it to come, whether for correction, or for his land, or for mercy.

¹⁴ 'Hearken unto this, O Job: stand still, and consider the wondrous works of God. ¹⁵ Dost thou know when God disposed them, and caused the light of his cloud to shine? ¹⁶ Dost thou know the balancings of the clouds, the wondrous works of him which is perfect in knowledge? ¹⁷ How thy garments are warm, when he quieteth the earth by the south wind? ¹⁸ Hast thou with him spread out the sky, which is strong, and as a molten looking glass? ¹⁹ Teach us what we shall say

unto him; for we cannot order our speech by reason of darkness. ²⁰ Shall it be told him that I speak? If a man speak,
surely he shall be swallowed up. ²¹ And now men see not the
bright light which is in the clouds; but the wind passeth, and
cleanseth them. ²² Fair weather cometh out of the north; with
God is terrible majesty. ²³ Touching the Almighty, we cannot
find him out; he is excellent in power, and in judg-ment, and
in plenty of justice; he will not afflict. ²⁴ Men do therefore fear
him; he respecteth not any that are wise of heart.'

38 Then the Lord answered Job out of the whirlwind, and said,

²'Who is this that darkeneth counsel by words
   without knowledge?
³ Gird up now thy loins like a man;
   for I will demand of thee, and answer thou me.
⁴ Where wast thou when I laid
   the foundations of the earth?
      Declare, if thou hast understanding.
⁵ Who hath laid the measures thereof,
   if thou knowest?
      Or who hath stretched the line upon it?
⁶ Whereupon are the foundations thereof fastened?
   Or who laid the corner stone thereof,
⁷ when the morning stars sang together,
   and all the sons of God shouted for joy?
⁸ Or who shut up the sea with doors,

when it brake forth,
as if it had issued out of the womb,
⁹ when I made the cloud the garment thereof,
and thick darkness a swaddling-band for it,
¹⁰ and brake up for it my decreed place,
and set bars and doors,
¹¹ and said, "Hitherto shalt thou come, but no further:
and here shall thy proud waves be stayed"?
¹² Hast thou commanded the morning since thy days,
and caused the dayspring to know his place;
¹³ that it might take hold of the ends of the earth,
that the wicked might be shaken out of it?
¹⁴ It is turned as clay to the seal;
and they stand as a garment.
¹⁵ And from the wicked their light is withholden,
and the high arm shall be broken.
¹⁶ Hast thou entered into the springs of the sea?
Or hast thou walked in the search of the depth?
¹⁷ Have the gates of death been opened unto thee?
Or hast thou seen the doors of
the shadow of death?
¹⁸ Hast thou perceived the breadth of the earth?
Declare if thou knowest it all.
¹⁹ Where is the way where light dwelleth?
And as for darkness, where is the place thereof,
²⁰ that thou shouldest take it to the bound thereof,
and that thou shouldest know the paths
to the house thereof?

²¹ Knowest thou it, because thou wast then born?
  Or because the number of thy days is great?
²² Hast thou entered into the treasures of the snow?
  Or hast thou seen the treasures of the hail,
²³ which I have reserved against the time of trouble,
  against the day of battle and war?
²⁴ By what way is the light parted,
  which scattereth the east wind upon the earth?
²⁵ Who hath divided a watercourse
  for the overflowing of waters,
    or a way for the lightning of thunder;
²⁶ to cause it to rain on the earth, where no man is;
  on the wilderness, wherein there is no man;
²⁷ to satisfy the desolate and waste ground;
  and to cause the bud of the tender herb
    to spring forth?
²⁸ Hath the rain a father?
  Or who hath begotten the drops of dew?
²⁹ Out of whose womb came the ice?
  And the hoary frost of heaven,
    who hath gendered it?
³⁰ The waters are hid as with a stone,
  and the face of the deep is frozen.
³¹ Canst thou bind the sweet influences of Pleiades,
  or loose the bands of Orion?
³² Canst thou bring forth Mazzaroth in his season?
  Or canst thou guide Arcturus with his sons?
³³ Knowest thou the ordinances of heaven?

Canst thou set the dominion thereof in the earth?
³⁴ Canst thou lift up thy voice to the clouds,
  that abundance of waters may cover thee? .
³⁵ Canst thou send lightnings, that they may go,
  and say unto thee, "Here we are"?
³⁶ Who hath put wisdom in the inward parts?
  Or who hath given understanding to the heart?
³⁷ Who can number the clouds in wisdom?
  Or who can stay the bottles of heaven,
³⁸ when the dust groweth into hardness,
  and the clods cleave fast together?
³⁹ Wilt thou hunt the prey for the lion,
  or fill the appetite of the young lions,
⁴⁰ when they couch in their dens,
  and abide in the covert to lie in wait?
⁴¹ Who provideth for the raven his food
  when his young ones cry unto God,
    they wander for lack of meat.'

39 'Knowest thou the time when the wild goats of
    the rock bring forth?
      Or canst thou mark when the hinds do calve?
² Canst thou number the months that they fulfil?
  Or knowest thou the time when they bring forth?
³ They bow themselves,
    they bring forth their young ones,
      they cast out their sorrows.
⁴ Their young ones are in good liking,

they grow up with corn;

    they go forth, and return not unto them.

⁵ Who hath sent out the wild ass free?

    Or who hath loosed the bands of the wild ass

⁶ whose house I have made the wilderness,

    and the barren land his dwellings?

⁷ He scorneth the multitude of the city,

    neither regardeth he the crying of the driver.

⁸ The range of the mountains is his pasture,

    and he searcheth after every green thing.

⁹ Will the unicorn be willing to serve thee,

    or abide by the crib?

¹⁰ Canst thou bind the unicorn

    with his band in the furrow?

      Or will he harrow the valleys after thee?

¹¹ Wilt thou trust him, because his strength is great?

    Or wilt thou leave thy labour to him?

¹² Wilt thou believe him,

    that he will bring home thy seed,

      and gather it into thy barn?

¹³ Gavest thou the goodly wings unto the peacocks

    or wings and feathers unto the ostrich

¹⁴ which leaveth her eggs in the earth,

    and warmeth them in dust,

¹⁵ and forgetteth that the foot may crush them,

    or that the wild beast may break them?

¹⁶ She is hardened against her young ones,

    as though they were not hers;

her labour is in vain without fear,

¹⁷ because God hath deprived her of wisdom,
neither hath he imparted to her understanding.

¹⁸ What time she lifteth up herself on high,
she scorneth the horse and his rider.

¹⁹ Hast thou given the horse strength?
Hast thou clothed his neck with thunder?

²⁰ Canst thou make him afraid as a grasshopper?
The glory of his nostrils is terrible.

²¹ He paweth in the valley,
and rejoiceth in his strength;
he goeth on to meet the armed men.

²² He mocketh at fear, and is not affrighted;
neither turneth he back from the sword.

²³ The quiver rattleth against him,
the glittering spear and the shield.

²⁴ He swalloweth the ground with fierceness and rage;
neither believeth he
that it is the sound of the trumpet.

²⁵ He saith among the trumpets, "Ha, ha;"
and he smelleth the battle afar off,
the thunder of the captains, and the shouting.

²⁶ Doth the hawk fly by thy wisdom,
and stretch her wings toward the south?

²⁷ Doth the eagle mount up at thy command,
and make her nest on high?

²⁸ She dwelleth and abideth on the rock,
upon the crag of the rock, and the strong place.

²⁹ From thence she seeketh the prey,
and her eyes behold afar off.
³⁰ Her young ones also suck up blood;
and where the slain are, there is she.'

40

Moreover the Lord answered Job, and said,

² 'Shall he that contendeth with the Almighty
instruct him?
He that reproveth God, let him answer it.'

³ Then Job answered the Lord, and said,

⁴ 'Behold, I am vile; what shall I answer thee?
I will lay mine hand upon my mouth.
⁵ Once have I spoken, but I will not answer;
yea, twice, but I will proceed no further.'

⁶ Then answered the Lord unto Job out of the whirlwind,
and said,

⁷ 'Gird up thy loins now like a man;
I will demand of thee, and declare thou unto me.
⁸ Wilt thou also disannul my judgment?
Wilt thou condemn me,
that thou mayest be righteous?
⁹ Hast thou an arm like God?
Or canst thou thunder with a voice like him?
¹⁰ Deck thyself now with majesty and excellency;
and array thyself with glory and beauty.

¹¹ Cast abroad the rage of thy wrath:
  and behold every one that is proud,
    and abase him.
¹² Look on every one that is proud,
  and bring him low;
    and tread down the wicked in their place.
¹³ Hide them in the dust together;
  and bind their faces in secret.
¹⁴ Then will I also confess unto thee
  that thine own right hand can save thee.
¹⁵ Behold now behemoth, which I made with thee;
  he eateth grass as an ox.
¹⁶ Lo now, his strength is in his loins,
  and his force is in the navel of his belly.
¹⁷ He moveth his tail like a cedar:
  the sinews of his stones are wrapped together.
¹⁸ His bones are as strong pieces of brass;
  his bones are like bars of iron.
¹⁹ He is the chief of the ways of God;
  he that made him can make his sword
    to approach unto him.
²⁰ Surely the mountains bring him forth food,
  where all the beasts of the field play.
²¹ He lieth under the shady trees,
  in the covert of the reed, and fens.
²² The shady trees cover him with their shadow;
  the willows of the brook compass him about.
²³ Behold, he drinketh up a river, and hasteth not;

he trusteth that he can draw up Jordan
    into his mouth.
²⁴ He taketh it with his eyes;
    his nose pierceth through snares.'

41 'Canst thou draw out leviathan with an hook?
    Or his tongue with a cord which thou lettest down?
² Canst thou put an hook into his nose?
    Or bore his jaw through with a thorn?
³ Will he make many supplications unto thee?
    Will he speak soft words unto thee?
⁴ Will he make a covenant with thee?
    Wilt thou take him for a servant for ever?
⁵ Wilt thou play with him as with a bird?
    Or wilt thou bind him for thy maidens?
⁶ Shall the companions make a banquet of him?
    Shall they part him among the merchants?
⁷ Canst thou fill his skin with barbed irons
    or his head with fish spears?
⁸ Lay thine hand upon him,
    remember the battle, do no more.
⁹ Behold, the hope of him is in vain; shall not one
    be cast down even at the sight of him?
¹⁰ None is so fierce that dare stir him up;
    who then is able to stand before me?
¹¹ Who hath prevented me, that I should repay him?
    Whatsoever is under the whole heaven is mine.
¹² I will not conceal his parts, nor his power,

nor his comely proportion.
¹³ Who can discover the face of his garment?
Or who can come to him with his double bridle?
¹⁴ Who can open the doors of his face?
His teeth are terrible round about.
¹⁵ His scales are his pride, shut up together
as with a close seal.
¹⁶ One is so near to another,
that no air can come between them.
¹⁷ They are joined one to another, they stick together,
that they cannot be sundered.
¹⁸ By his neesings a light doth shine,
and his eyes are like the eyelids of the morning.
¹⁹ Out of his mouth go burning lamps,
and sparks of fire leap out.
²⁰ Out of his nostrils goeth smoke,
as out of a seething pot or caldron.
²¹ His breath kindleth coals,
and a flame goeth out of his mouth.
²² In his neck remaineth strength,
and sorrow is turned into joy before him.
²³ The flakes of his flesh are joined together;
they are firm in themselves;
they cannot be moved.
²⁴ His heart is as firm as a stone;
yea, as hard as a piece of the nether millstone.
²⁵ When he raiseth up himself, the mighty are afraid;
by reason of breakings they purify themselves.

²⁶ The sword of him that layeth at him cannot hold
   the spear, the dart, nor the habergeon.
²⁷ He esteemeth iron as straw,
   and brass as rotten wood.
²⁸ The arrow cannot make him flee;
   slingstones are turned with him into stubble.
²⁹ Darts are counted as stubble;
   he laugheth at the shaking of a spear.
³⁰ Sharp stones are under him;
   he spreadeth sharp pointed things upon the mire.
³¹ He maketh the deep to boil like a pot;
   he maketh the sea like a pot of ointment.
³² He maketh a path to shine after him;
   one would think the deep to be hoary.
³³ Upon earth there is not his like,
   who is made without fear.
³⁴ He beholdeth all high things;
   he is a king over all the children of pride.'

42 Then Job answered the Lord, and said,

² 'I know that thou canst do every thing,
   and that no thought can be withholden from thee.
³ Who is he that hideth counsel without knowledge?
   Therefore have I uttered that I understood not;
      things too wonderful for me,
   which I knew not.
⁴ Hear, I beseech thee, and I will speak;

I will demand of thee, and declare thou unto me.
⁵ I have heard of thee by the hearing of the ear;
   but now mine eye seeth thee.
⁶ Wherefore I abhor myself,
   and repent in dust and ashes.'

⁷ And it was so, that after the Lord had spoken these words unto Job, the Lord said to Eliphaz the Temanite, 'My wrath is kindled against thee, and against thy two friends; for ye have not spoken of me the thing that is right, as my servant Job hath. ⁸ Therefore take unto you now seven bullocks and seven rams, and go to my servant Job, and offer up for yourselves a burnt offering; and my servant Job shall pray for you, for him will I accept lest I deal with you after your folly, in that ye have not spoken of me the thing which is right, like my servant Job.' ⁹ So Eliphaz the Temanite and Bildad the Shuhite and Zophar the Naamathite went, and did according as the Lord commanded them; the Lord also accepted Job.

¹⁰ And the Lord turned the captivity of Job, when he prayed for his friends; also the Lord gave Job twice as much as he had before. ¹¹ Then came there unto him all his brethren, and all his sisters, and all they that had been of his acquaintance before, and did eat bread with him in his house; and they bemoaned him, and comforted him over all the evil that the Lord had brought upon him; every man also gave him a piece of money, and every one an earring of gold. ¹² So the Lord blessed the latter end of Job more than his beginning; for he had fourteen thousand sheep, and six thousand camels, and a

thousand yoke of oxen, and a thousand she asses. ¹³He had also seven sons and three daughters. ¹⁴And he called the name of the first Jemima; and the name of the second Kezia; and the name of the third Kerenhappuch. ¹⁵And in all the land were no women found so fair as the daughters of Job; and their father gave them inheritance among their brethren. ¹⁶After this lived Job an hundred and forty years, and saw his sons, and his sons' sons, even four generations. ¹⁷So Job died, being old and full of days.